LAS VEGAS ☀ SUN

T0312819

PROMISE

FULFILLED

HOW THE VEGAS GOLDEN KNIGHTS CONQUERED THEIR STANLEY CUP QUEST

SPECIAL COMMEMORATIVE BOOK

LAS VEGAS ☀ SUN

Brian Greenspun, CEO, Publisher and Editor
Robert Cauthorn, Chief Operating Officer
Ray Brewer, Managing Editor
Dave Mondt, Managing Editor/News
John Taylor, Copy Chief
Corlene Byrd, Art Director
Case Keefer, Assistant Sports Editor
Danny Webster, Golden Knights Beat Writer
Abe Kobylanski, Copy Editor
Andy Lefkowitz, Copy Editor
Steve Marcus, Photographer
Wade Vandervort, Photographer
Brian Ramos, Photo Coordinator

Copyright © 2023 Las Vegas Sun

No part of this publication may be reproduced, stored in a retrieval system or transmitted in any form by any means,
electronic, mechanical, photocopying or otherwise, without prior written permission of the publisher,
Triumph Books LLC, 814 North Franklin Street; Chicago, Illinois 60610.

This book is available in quantity at special discounts for your group or organization.
For further information, contact:

Triumph Books LLC
814 North Franklin Street
Chicago, Illinois 60610
Phone: (312) 337-0747
www.triumphbooks.com

Printed in U.S.A.
ISBN: 978-1-63727-364-7

Content packaged by Mojo Media, Inc.
Joe Funk: Editor
Jason Hinman: Creative Director

Front cover photos by AP Images (Jonathan Marchessault) and Steve Marcus / Las Vegas Sun (William Karlsson and Mark Stone)
Back cover photo by Steve Marcus / Las Vegas Sun

This is an unofficial publication. This book is in no way affiliated with, licensed by or endorsed by
the Vegas Golden Knights, the National Hockey League or any associated entities.

CONTENTS

INTRODUCTION

By Case Keefer

The term "Cup in Six" is no longer a cute catchphrase to describe the outsized ambitions of the nascent local NHL franchise.

It's a premonition realized. A championship claimed. A promise fulfilled.

The Vegas Golden Knights lifted the Stanley Cup at T-Mobile Arena after blowing out the Florida Panthers 9-3 in Game 5.

Forward Mark Stone scored his first of three goals 12 minutes into the game, giving Vegas a 1-0 lead despite Florida having mostly controlled the puck early on. The deluge came soon thereafter, and the Golden Knights went into the second intermission up 6-1 after Stone wristed in his second goal.

"It was a pretty slow start," Stone said during the second break on the team's radio broadcast. "I don't know if it was nervous energy or what, but we turned it on."

Because of his role as captain, Stone was the first to touch the Stanley Cup, or what he and his teammates have referred to as "the ultimate prize" throughout the postseason. The first NHL championship in franchise history appropriately came in the franchise's sixth year, just as owner Bill Foley targeted upon being awarded the league's 31st team in June 2016.

Foley was talking about winning a title by the sixth year before the team even had a name, let alone any personnel. But he immediately started putting people in the right positions to make that possible, including in the front office where two of his first hires were current President of Hockey Operations George McPhee and General Manager Kelly McCrimmon.

The duo succeeded wildly in June 2017's expansion draft, putting together a group of players that reached the Stanley Cup Final in June 2018 before losing in five games to the Washington Capitals. But that initial team laid the groundwork and continued to exert its influence all the way into this year's championship run.

Original Golden Knight Jonathan Marchessault, who was acquired from the Panthers in the expansion draft, won the Conn Smythe Trophy as the most valuable player in this year's Stanley Cup Playoffs.

Marchessault assisted on the Golden Knights' second goal in the clinching game, a close-range tap-in by Nicolas Hague, to set a franchise record with 25 playoff points this season — 13 goals and 12 assists.

The team's second-leading goal-scorer throughout the playoffs was fellow original Golden Knight William Karlsson, who found the net 11 times. In an ode to the Golden Knights' history, coach Bruce Cassidy started a lineup of Marchessault, Karlsson, forward Reilly Smith, defenseman Shea Theodore and defenseman Brayden McNabb in Game 5.

Smith scored, assisted by Karlsson and Theodore, as part of the second-period onslaught.

Forward William Carrier and defenseman Zach Whitecloud were the two other players crowned champions after being with the Golden Knights since the team's first season.

But Vegas would never have delivered on Foley's

wish if not for an aggressive, oftentimes controversial strategy of adding the best possible talent to the roster over the years. All of those big-ticket acquisitions seemed to coalesce this playoff run, overcoming unique hardships and navigating outside criticism to prove their championship caliber.

The 31-year-old Stone has been Vegas' best two-way player since arriving via a trade deadline deal with the Ottawa Senators in 2019, but he's recently struggled with back problems.

Stone was unsure if he'd even appear in the 2023 playoffs after being assigned to long-term injured reserve and undergoing back surgery in February — his second operation in less than a year.

But he rehabbed relentlessly and was able to return for the entire playoff run. He got his Game 5 hat trick on an empty-netter with about six minutes left to play, sending the record T-Mobile Arena crowd of 19,058 into a complete frenzy.

"He's unbelievable," teammate Jack Eichel said of Stone during intermission on the radio broadcast. "He's so good at everything, and he does it every day."

Eichel, the Golden Knights' other frontline star, came to Vegas in a midseason trade in late 2021 and immediately underwent neck surgery that his original team, the Buffalo Sabres, had vehemently opposed. Unfairly besmirched as entitled and egocentric in Buffalo, the 26-year-old eradicated the narrative in his first career appearance in the playoffs this season.

He even looked too unselfish at times, putting his scoring acumen on the back burner to lead the NHL with 20 playoff assists, including a trio in the deciding win.

Vegas was proudly a defense-first team all year, and no one instilled that mentality better than top-pair blue-liner Alex Pietrangelo, who signed with the team in free agency before the 2020-2021 season. Pietrangelo proved the perfect fit in the preferred system of Cassidy, who arrived in Vegas this season after being unceremoniously fired after six years with the Boston Bruins this postseason.

Adin Hill was similarly easy to obtain. The Golden Knights traded for him shortly before the start of the season, when a rash of injuries (to planned starter Robin Lehner and backup Laurent Brossoit) left them thin at goaltender. The 27-year-old may have begun as the team's fourth choice in the crease, but injuries elevated him to No. 1 midway through the playoffs, and he looked the part.

He led all qualified goalies in the playoffs with a .934 save percentage and managed 31 saves in Game 5. The Panthers, even without injured star Matthew Tkachuk, peppered him with several chances in the opening 10 minutes, but Hill stood strong.

The Golden Knights' touted their depth all season, a strength that also came through in the deciding game. Role players like Hague, Nic Roy and Michael Amadio all had goals, as did recent trade acquisition Ivan Barbashev and defenseman Alec Martinez.

"We balance minutes," Cassidy said about what makes his team special. "It starts there. We try not to overtax any one individual."

Between the unproven players down the lineup, goalie uncertainty, new-coach questions and big-name injuries, the Golden Knights came into the season as the longest shot they've been to win the Cup since their very first year. Future prices in local sports books reached as high as 25-to-1, but those odds must not have factored in the destiny it felt like Foley's words unleashed.

"Cup in Six" was already one of the boldest proclamations in hockey history, but now it's also one of the most accurate. The Golden Knights are Stanley Cup champions. ∎

CAN'T HANDLE VEGAS

Golden Knights Brought the Flash, Panthers Acted Like Trash in Game 1

By Case Keefer

Some guys just can't handle Vegas.

It's one of the most overused clichés about our city, but hear me out. What theory better explains how the Florida Panthers acted in Game 1 of the Stanley Cup Final?

Florida reached this year's championship matchup as a feel-good story that continually defied the odds and pulled three straight playoff series upsets to win the Eastern Conference crown. The Panthers did so by continually keeping their cool despite any and all circumstances, which allowed them to come through in the biggest moments.

There was no semblance of that identity in their 5-2 loss to the Golden Knights at T-Mobile Arena. Florida played like a group of goons for most of the game, and then got worse when things didn't go its way late — elevating into a consortium of cheap-shot artists.

"Everybody just (expletive) breathe," Florida coach Paul Maurice said with a smirk after the game. "I feel like you people have been here; you're tight."

Too bad Maurice apparently didn't dispense that advice to his team on the bench in the third period instead of to media members in a postgame interview room.

The Panthers' best player, Matthew Tkachuk, could have used some spur-of-the-moment meditation practice before punching defenseless Vegas blue-liner Nicolas Hague in the face twice to get a late game-misconduct penalty. The officials also tossed fellow Florida forward Sam Bennett in the same skirmish, while Vegas' Chandler Stephenson met the same fate for reasons unknown.

The score was 4-2 with about five minutes to play when those tempers flared, enough time for the Panthers to conceivably pull out the type of miracle they've managed multiple times throughout the playoffs. They even conveniently got a breakaway chance seconds later, but Vegas goalie Adin Hill waited out Florida forward Sam Reinhardt to force a wrister wide of the net.

Golden Knight Reilly Smith scored an empty-netter when the puck went back the other way, getting slashed by Panther defenseman Radko Gudas for another penalty in the aftermath.

"We played our composed game," Vegas forward Jonathan Marchessault said. "We didn't get too heated like they did at the end. I think that's winning hockey for us."

A little Vegas flash was all it took to take Florida out of its element. The Golden Knights certainly brought the glitz in rising to the occasion for the opener of their second Stanley Cup Final in franchise history.

Zach Whitecloud celebrates after giving the Golden Knights the lead with a third-period goal. (Steve Marcus / Las Vegas Sun)

The third-period game-winning goal where third-pair defensemen Zach Whitecloud surprised even coach Bruce Cassidy by sliding into the slot for a wrister was probably their least showy score.

A first-period snipe by Marchessault, second-period shimmy-then-slap by defenseman Shea Theodore and a third-period knock-down-and-fire by captain Mark Stone were among the Golden Knights' most dazzling goals of the postseason. Stone's score was set up by a Tkachuk turnover a few minutes before his ejection so there were reasons to explain the latter's frustration.

But more must be expected out of a Stanley Cup Final team's superstar player. Even if the Panthers felt like some extracurricular physicality was necessary, Tkachuk should have let someone else do the dirty work.

Don't have the player upon whom the franchise must rely to eventually win the series mess with someone like Hague, a 6-foot-6, 230-pound mountain.

"Our team has stuck together all year," said Vegas forward Jack Eichel, who rushed in to try to get Tkachuk away from Hague. "We do a good job of standing up for each other and I think that's something we take a lot of pride in. We know it's going to be physical."

Florida's agitation was most evident at the end of the game, but there were glimmers throughout the first 55 minutes of play too. Former Golden Knight Nick Cousins appeared to have a consistent bone to pick with chippy play throughout including an early roughing penalty on Hill.

Vegas' goalie was a particular source of frustration for Florida. Hill stopped two consecutive close-range shots by Bennett in the middle of the second period, and the Panthers immediately started shoving when the goalie gloved the second one.

The Golden Knights were the adults in the room.

"We do have a veteran group and I think it showed late in the game when we were sort of able to keep our discipline and get to the finish line," Cassidy said.

In fairness, the Golden Knights had an uncharacteristic meltdown of their own during this playoff run. Alternate captain Alex Pietrangelo's slash on Leon Draisaitl at the end of a Game 4 loss to the Edmonton Oilers was worse as a singular moment than anything the Panthers pulled.

Many expected the Golden Knights to lose the series when he was suspended for the next game, but they bounced back to win two straight and move on to the Western Conference Final. Tkachuk is highly unlikely to, and shouldn't be, suspended so there's an even better chance for the Panthers to redeem themselves.

But it's not going to happen if they carry themselves like they did in Game 1.

It's not going to happen if they keep acting like belligerent tourists who think the normal rules don't apply in Vegas.

"We're just trying to play the right way and be disciplined," Marchessault said. "Tonight, we were able to be the better team." ∎

Shea Theodore scored in the second period with assists from Brayden McNabb and Brett Howden. (AP Images)

CreditOne
CreditOne
27
CCM
21
CCM
Circa SPORTS
Circa SPORTS

STAY HUNGRY

Past Heartbreak Has Fueled the Golden Knights to a 2-0 Advantage

By Case Keefer

Bruce Cassidy's face turned red as he tried to scream at his team over one of the loudest crowds in T-Mobile Arena history during Game 2 of the Stanley Cup Final.

The Vegas Golden Knights had taken a 4-0 lead over the Florida Panthers with goals from Jonathan Marchessault, Alec Martinez, Nicolas Roy and Brett Howden, but this was not the look of a coach in the midst of a victory that would take his franchise closer to a championship than it had ever been before. Cassidy appeared generally alarmed, concerned that his players had gotten lost in the emotion of the moment and desperately attempting to steer them back on course.

"There were some parts there where we lost our competitive edge for some shifts," Cassidy said during his postgame news conference later in the night. "You've got to be real careful this time of the year. This is not a January game where a team is moving on to their next opponent and so are we. We talked about that in between periods."

The Golden Knights gave up a goal 14 seconds into the third period but recovered to outscore the Panthers for a fourth consecutive period overall in the series. A 7-2 victory gave Vegas a 2-0 series lead heading to Sunrise, Florida, for Game 3 against the Panthers.

Still, Cassidy's near-panic despite what looked like a commanding lead felt emblematic of the Golden Knights' whole current playoff run. Vegas has fought against feeling comfortable, and tried to maintain a mentality that nothing will be good enough until it hoists the Stanley Cup.

The team declined to touch the Clarence S. Campbell Bowl awarded for winning the Western Conference, unlike when they won it the first time in 2018. After beating the Panthers 5-2 in Game 1 of this Cup Final, forward Jonathan Marchessault took borderline offense to a reporter in the locker room asking him how it felt to win a Stanley Cup Final game.

He had done that before, Marchessault said, in reference to 2018's Game 1 win over the Washington Capitals, but that series didn't turn out the way he wanted, with the Golden Knights losing in five games. No one dared to ask Marchessault a similar question in a postgame news conference after Game 2, but he still repeated the same message he has shared all postseason.

"We've done a great job so far, but we're still pretty far from our goal," he said.

The path for a team down 2-0 getting back into a best-of-seven championship series is pretty well established. The trailing team must come out scorching

Brett Howden (21) scores against Panthers goaltender Alex Lyon to cap the Golden Knights' 7-2 win.
(Steve Marcus / Las Vegas Sun)

in Game 3 with a desperation its opponent cannot match, build from there and prolong the series.

The Golden Knights seem unlikely to succumb to that fate. That's not to say that they can't lose Game 3, or even the series; just that, if they do so, complacency won't be a contributing factor.

Vegas is too hungry, and Cassidy has it too locked in, because of what has happened in the past. Between the Cup Final to end the Golden Knights' inaugural season, a painful loss to San Jose in Round 1 the following year and two series upset defeats in the Western Conference Final in 2020 and '21, they're keenly aware of the consequences of even briefly losing focus.

"It's unfinished business for a lot of guys," Cassidy said hours before Game 1. "I put myself in that category."

Perhaps Cassidy's drive for Cup redemption is part of the reason why he has fit so well with the Golden Knights in his first year as coach. His previous disappointment didn't come behind the Vegas bench, but it stung just as much when his Boston Bruins' teams fell short in the playoffs in each of the past six years.

Cassidy's best Boston squad held a 2-1 lead in the 2019 Cup Final before getting upset by the St. Louis Blues in seven games. The coach has admitted to thinking about the defeat frequently in the years since.

Cassidy says he's confident he did all he could schematically to give the Bruins the best chance to win, but he wonders if he handled the increased outside obligations during the series as well as he could have. Should he have been more stringent about keeping Boston on its normal routine? And did he truly realize how rarely championship opportunities present themselves?

"I think the first time around I [had] only [been] at it [in Boston] for three years, and it was like, 'Wow, the Stanley Cup Final, it's kinda cool,'" Cassidy reflected. "Now, I've been to the Stanley Cup Final, and it's time to win it.

"I'm not saying I wasn't prepared or trying to win it last time. I just think you have a different mindset once you go through the whole process, when you get near the top of the hill but not quite to the top."

Cassidy's Vegas players know that feeling, too. It would be easy for them to point out that every season features a different team, separating this year's run from past attempts at the Cup. But players like Marchessault haven't given that excuse any credence.

The Golden Knights have accomplished almost everything in their first six seasons, including an NHL-leading 12 playoff series wins, but there's a void that will only grow bigger if they can't defeat the Panthers two more times.

Hockey can be so crazy and unpredictable, it would be a mistake to discount the chances of a comeback. But Florida will have it to pry it away from the Golden Knights, whose grip is hardened after years of painful strengthening.

"Unfinished business is a good way to put it," defenseman Zach Whitecloud said. "Everyone who follows this team knows we've come into this season with a chip on our shoulder and with something to prove not only to ourselves but to our fanbase and the rest of the league." ■

Jonathan Marchessault led the charge for Vegas in Game 2 with two goals and one assist. (Steve Marcus / Las Vegas Sun)

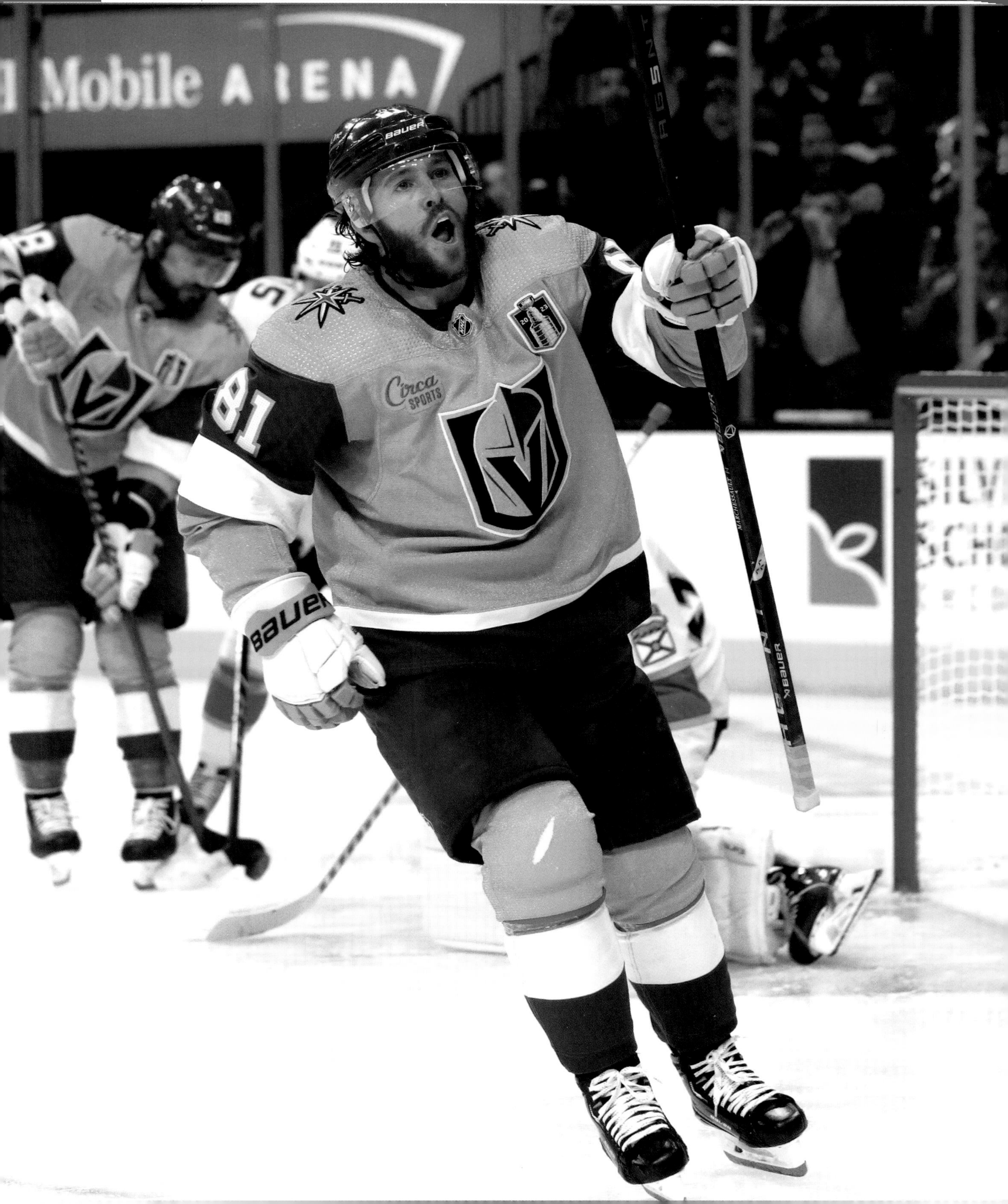
Mobile ARENA
BAUER
Circa SPORTS
81
BAUER

A TOUGH PILL TO SWALLOW

Vegas Eager to Move On from Missed Opportunity in Game 3

By Danny Webster

You wouldn't think the Golden Knights just let a potential 3-0 series lead in the Stanley Cup Final slip through their fingers upon entering the locker room. The Vegas leadership group stood front and center trying to assure that everything is fine moments after squandering a late third-period lead, then losing in overtime to allow the Florida Panthers back in the series.

It will be a tough pill to swallow for the night with the Golden Knights two minutes away from a commanding series lead, only for Matthew Tkachuk to tie it in the third and Carter Verhaeghe to send it home in overtime and give the Panthers a 3-2 win in Game 3 of the Cup Final at FLA Live Arena.

Instead of that 3-0 lead, Vegas holds a 2-1 lead now with Game 4 to come in Sunrise.

"Overall, I thought we played a pretty solid game," said captain Mark Stone. "It's the playoffs. You've got to bounce back and be ready for the next one."

Stone is right. Playoff hockey determines two things: Which team is clicking at the right time, and which team can get the bounces to go its way.

The Golden Knights did everything right to prevent those bounces. Even after giving up the game's first goal to Brandon Montour 4:08 into the game, the Golden Knights' composure playing on the road has been a strength throughout the playoffs.

They got that response on the power play at 16:03 when Stone scored his first road goal of the playoffs on a deflection from a shot by Jonathan Marchessault, tying it 1-1.

Shot numbers would indicate the Golden Knights were dominated in the opening 20, and giving up the attempts advantage 19-7 to Florida would affirm that. Yet despite Florida controlling the early going with its forecheck and sustained pressure, coach Bruce Cassidy felt they played well in the period sans giving up the opening goal.

"I think we gave up five shots. We figured we might have to chase it a little bit in terms of the energy in the building," Cassidy said. "There's a lot to like about our game tonight."

That momentum carried into the second where Vegas controlled play with its forecheck and continuous denial of zone entries. Though each team had three penalties in the second, the Golden Knights were the ones to capitalize when Jonathan Marchessault scored his 13th goal of the postseason for a 2-1 Vegas lead.

The Golden Knights played as good of a defensive game as you could want from a road team. They held the Panthers to 17 shots on goal for 57-plus minutes. They had a 31-17 edge in blocked shots. Vegas took away nearly every inch of room in the middle of the ice to limit high-danger chances for Florida.

One of two things were going to happen, given the trajectory of the Golden Knights' postseason run: Either they would score that third goal, improve to 15-0 in the playoffs when scoring three goals, or find a way to let it go. The middle ground is nonexistent.

When Tkachuk tied it 2-2 with 2:13 remaining with the extra attacker after pulling Sergei Bobrovsky, the narrative continued.

Tkachuk was likely laboring throughout the game. He didn't play the last 12 minutes of the first after a hit by Keegan Kolesar prompted the NHL's concussion spotters to check him out, Panthers coach Paul Maurice confirmed after the game. Tkachuk didn't even start the second period, only to appear a few minutes later.

The Panthers weren't going to get back into the Cup Final without Tkachuk, who has spent more time off the ice and in the penalty box than making an impact on it. With his 11th goal of the playoffs, Tkachuk made his presence felt in a good way for the Panthers.

"It's not always going to be perfect," defenseman Alex Pietrangelo said. "It was a good push by them. We would've loved to win that. I thought we did a lot of good things throughout the game. We didn't start great, but we got to our game as the game progressed."

Verhaeghe's shot 4:27 into overtime was a product of the Golden Knights allowing too much center ice and Verhaeghe getting a good look. Tkachuk was in front,

but he claims he didn't set the screen to shield Adin Hill from the puck beating him.

Yet, after all of that, the Golden Knights still feel comfortable with where they're at.

"You're up a goal with two minutes left, but it's all part of it," center Jack Eichel said. "I think our mindset shouldn't change. Every game is the most important game of the season. Just go out there and win the next one. That's the plan."

They also attribute to the three posts they hit — including Ivan Barbashev hitting the crossbar on a 2-on-1 late in the third period — signaling the opportunities were there, but just failed to capitalize.

"I hope it leaves a sour taste in your mouth, at least for the night," Cassidy said. "I hope they're upset with certain things that transpired, but it's OK. It's an emotional game, but not tomorrow. It can't be tomorrow."

Even in the rare victory of special teams, it was destined to be the Golden Knights' night. They went 2 for 5 on the power play and killed all five Panthers power plays to improve to 12 for 12 on the penalty kill this series.

Not even that was good enough to move one win away from the Stanley Cup.

Perhaps that's why the Golden Knights sent Stone, Pietrangelo and Eichel to speak to a flood of microphones in the locker room. The captain and two former captains all coming to an agreement that they can win Game 4 if they play the same way.

But the Panthers have momentum now. This is a series, and with one more home game upcoming, the underdogs — er, cats — of these playoffs still have a heartbeat.

"This series, we knew it was going to be tough," Stone said. "They're a resilient team. You're going to deal with close games, but we'll be ready for the next one." ■

HOLD THE LINE

Knights' Late-Game Resolve Has Them One Win Away from Stanley Cup

By Case Keefer

The fists and plastic rats flew as the final horn sounded FLA Live Arena to signal the end of Game 4 of the Stanley Cup Final. Both were aimed towards the Golden Knights' heads.

As well as Vegas had shown restraint against Florida's dirty tactics, and sometimes even literally laughed them off, throughout the series, the Golden Knights chose to protect themselves in this instance. They were going to stand their ground in a skirmish that developed right in front of, and swallowed up, goalie Adin Hill.

It was a fitting end to the Golden Knights' most intense game this season considering their determination at the net front is what led them to a 3-2 victory and one win away from lifting the Stanley Cup.

If they maintain the toughness they showed in fending off a barrage of shots over the final 2:30 of game time after the Panthers pulled goalie Sergei Bobrovsky, they'll be celebrating soon.

"Guys just sold out to get it done," captain Mark Stone said after Game 4. "We did a great job of making sure we held the line pretty well. We chipped pucks out when we needed to, we got clears and kept it outside to really compact the net front and did a good job making sure nothing really got around the net, not like last game."

The win tasted all the sweeter to the Golden Knights because of the way they prevailed in direct contrast to how they fared in the same situation in Game 3. The Panthers subbed out Bobrvosky for an extra skater at almost the exact same time on the clock that night, and they scored within seconds when Matthew Tkachuk was left uncovered in front of the net for a put-back goal.

The Golden Knights didn't feel like they played a bad game overall in Game 3, but coach Bruce Cassidy had two main gripes — That they failed in 5-on-6 play and weren't strong enough in front of the net for both Tkachuk's goal and Carter Verhaeghe's overtime winner.

The criticism turned to cheers.

"At the end, I wasn't thinking, 'Here we go again,'" Cassidy said in his postgame news conference. "We just went through it and one thing our team does well is we respond to adversity, or whatever hasn't gone well, and we've found a way to keep it out of our net. I don't know

Goaltender Adin Hill protects the net from a shot by Panthers center Sam Bennett (9) during the third period. Hill and the Golden Knights' defense held strong late in the game to maintain the narrow win. (AP Images)

if they had any Grade-As. They threw a few towards our net but I think we did a good job clearing them."

Hill was only forced to make one save over the first two minutes of the onslaught, when Tkachuk fired a puck through traffic. But then the final attempted clear went awry.

Top defenseman Alex Pietrangelo flung the puck over the glass, picking up a delay of game penalty to give Florida a 6-on-4 opportunity with 17 seconds to play.

Defensemen Zach Whitecloud and Brayden McNabb both blocked shots in the final sequence, with Hill turning away an attempt from Verhaeghe to end the game and start the brawl.

"I was just battling trying to find the puck and I guess there was a little mayhem after the buzzer there," Hill said. "But everyone on the ice there on our side did everything we could to keep the puck out of the net."

The big-time blocks weren't only at the end. Hill shouted out defenseman Alec Martinez for facing "a full slap shot, and taking it like a man" earlier in the third period.

Vegas finished with 30 blocks. The Golden Knights technically had one more in their previous contest, but most of them came earlier in the game.

They weren't in the right spots in the crucial moments at the end. And they weren't going to let that happen again.

"You learn from those situations," Pietrangelo said. "Is it always going to be perfect? No, last game, we gave up one...but you put that behind you and you move on to the next situation. That's what we did."

It wasn't only on defense that the Golden Knights strengthened on the inside. Cassidy thought the offense also could have been better in the middle and around the crease after Game 3.

Of course, the Golden Knights fixed it in Game 4.

Second-line center Chandler Stephenson was a slot machine, cashing in on a pair of goals right down the center of the ice in the opening period and a half to put the Golden Knights up 2-0. Then, from a similar spot, defenseman Nic Hague set up forward William Karlsson for a close-range snipe for a 3-0 advantage.

Vegas was so money up front that they scored the fourth goal too. Only problem was that it was for Florida.

With the Golden Knights packed in, a routine puck fling by Panthers defenseman Brandon Montour ricocheted off both McNabb's skate and defenseman Shea Theodore's ankle before finding the net.

"We got an unfortunate bounce there for them to get that one," Hill said. "But when we're rolling like that, we're the best team in the league."

There can be no debate about that with one more victory. T-Mobile Arena will be rocking like never before considering the series-clinching possibility.

If the notoriously thumping musical selections include Jimmy Eat World's "The Middle" like they have sometimes in the past, the song should probably be cranked up a couple more decibels. Resilient dominance in the middle and front of the ice is what's delivered the Golden Knights' playoff ride to within one victory of what they've been calling "the ultimate prize."

"The buzzer goes off and I felt my helmet get ripped off and they have six guys on the ice and we have four, so get in there and try to help out my teammates," Hill described the endgame situation. "I don't know if there's really a message to be sent. We're just getting ready for [Game 5]." ■

Chandler Stephenson scored a pair of early goals to give the Golden Knights a 2-0 lead. (AP Images)

STANLEY CUP CHAMPIONS

Golden Knights Capture the Ultimate Prize with Rout of Panthers

By Danny Webster

Bruce Cassidy walked his dog Winnie at around 11:30 a.m. the morning of Game 5. Other than the obvious reasons for taking a dog on a walk, two things would be accomplished on this trek: Cassidy would lower his anxiety, and he'd decide on his starting lineup in the biggest game in Golden Knights history.

Cassidy made up his mind to start five of the remaining six original Golden Knights — Jonathan Marchessault, William Karlsson, Reilly Smith, Brayden McNabb and Shea Theodore — in what would be the decisive game of the Stanley Cup Final. William Carrier got the short end of the stick, but he did receive a proper apology.

In front of the largest crowd ever for a Golden Knights game at T-Mobile Arena, the five received likely the loudest ovation ever heard during player introductions. One more time, the Misfit Line would skate together. This time, to finish the job they started six years ago.

Consider the final chapter finished.

Seven different players scored, including a historic hat trick from captain Mark Stone, to pave the way for a dominant 9-3 Golden Knights victory over the Florida Panthers to capture the first Stanley Cup in franchise history, coming in the sixth year of their existence.

"It got me all surprised. I didn't know we were going to start," Marchessault said. "It was a great gesture. Well-thought, and I didn't even think of it."

To put some cold water on this feel-good moment, not everyone thought it was a good idea. Golden Knights president of hockey operations George McPhee said it was a "bit of a gimmick, and we'd never done that sort of thing."

Perhaps that's a fair way to think of it, because the Golden Knights still needed to win one more game. If they lost, all the energy and anticipation heading into a close-out Game 5 would go to waste and the series would shift back to Florida.

But Cassidy felt it was the right call to give proper recognition to those who laid the foundation for what was to come in Las Vegas.

One of the six remaining Golden Knights who joined the team in the 2017 expansion draft, Jonathan Marchessault lifts the Stanley Cup following a dominant series against the Panthers. (Steve Marcus / Las Vegas Sun)

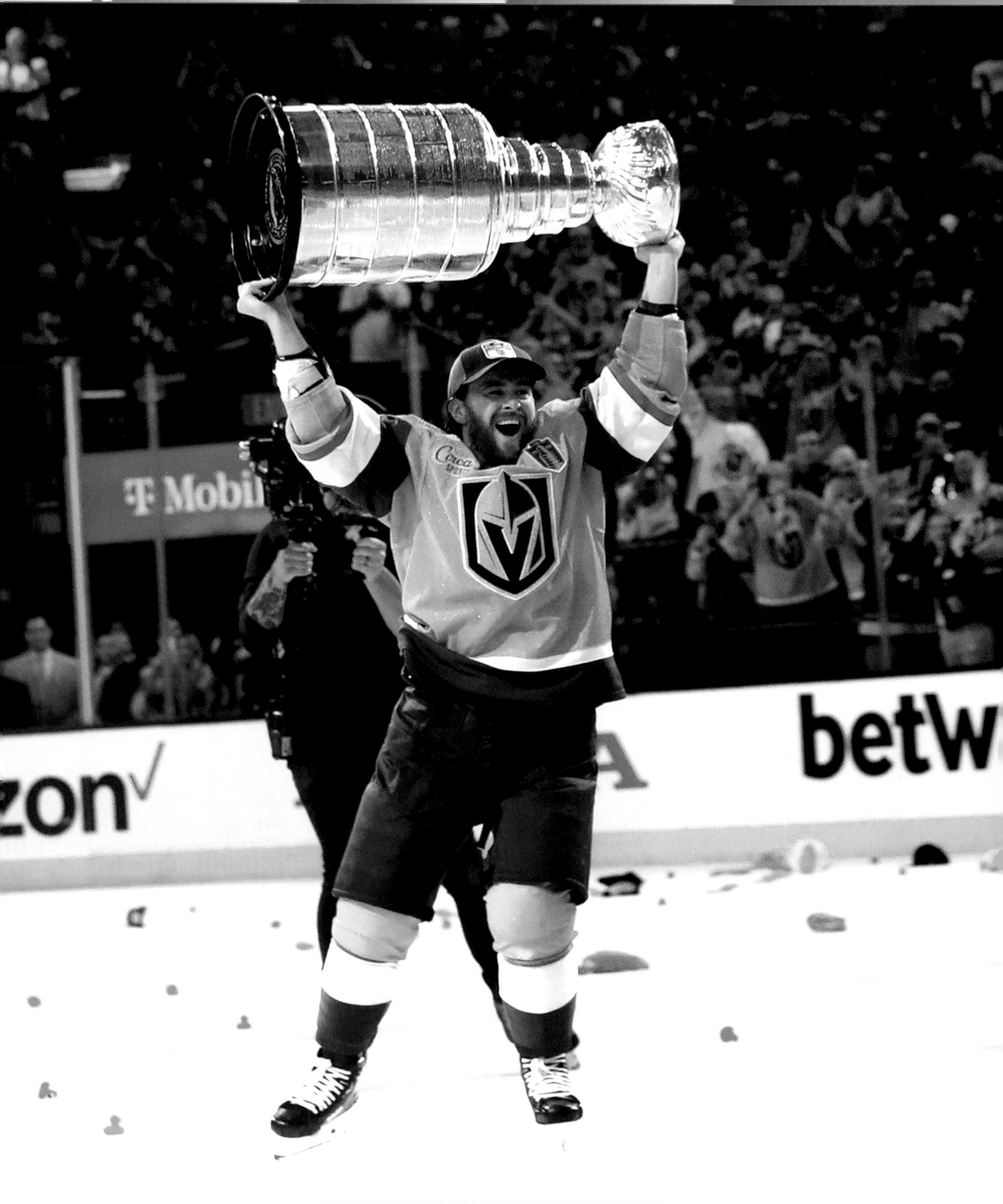
T Mobil
zon
betw

"I thought it would be nice and give us a little juice," Cassidy said. "Whether it did or not, I don't know, but they deserved it."

Cassidy won't be alone in thinking that.

On a night where Stone scored the first hat trick in a Stanley Cup Final since Peter Forsberg with the Colorado Avalanche in 1996 — also against the Panthers — he also acknowledged the contributions of the remaining six.

"Those guys, they mean a lot to this city," Stone said. "They've poured everything into this city and organization, and those guys are emotional players. It was pretty easy for us to jump on board with that."

Stone, as the captain, was the first to receive the Stanley Cup from NHL Commissioner Gary Bettman. After taking his victory lap with the 35-pound silver trophy, the first person Stone handed it to was Smith.

And then Marchessault, the Conn Smythe Trophy winner after a 25-point postseason (13 goals, 12 assists).

And then Karlsson.

Then McNabb, then Theodore, then Carrier.

Marchessault was given a slight heads up that Smith was going to get the Cup first, and then he was next in line.

"I was kind of shocked a little bit, because we have so many veterans in that locker room and guys who came in at different times the past six years and were huge for us," Marchessault said. "It was definitely a great gesture and something that will go down as one of the classiest things I've seen."

All six made some contribution in their own way to reach this point.

Karlsson's lost scoring touch returned in an emphatic way during the playoffs with 11 goals. Smith had 14 points (four goals, 10 assists) and was vital in the Golden Knights' team defense.

Jonathan Marchessault scored a record-tying 13 postseason goals, including finishing with a 10-game point streak, to earn the Conn Smythe Trophy. (Steve Marcus / Las Vegas Sun)

Carrier, who had a career-high 16 goals in 2022-23, missed the final month of the regular season with a lower-body injury, returned for Game 5 of the first round against Winnipeg and solidified the forward depth that carried the Golden Knights on a nightly basis.

McNabb remained a net-positive as a stay-at-home defenseman. Theodore struggled through the first two-and-a-half rounds, only to find his game against Dallas and finish with six points (one goal, five assists) in the Cup Final.

And then there's Marchessault, who did not have a goal in Vegas' first seven playoff games, only to finish with 13 — tying him with Edmonton's Leon Draisaitl for the most in the postseason — and conclude his run with a 10-game point streak (eight goals, seven assists).

Marchessault's journey — from an undrafted player, to 124 games in five years with three different teams, to being left unprotected in the expansion draft by these same Panthers — culminates in the acknowledgment of one of the best playoff performers over the last six years. He's already the all-time goals leader (150) and points leader (348) in Golden Knights history.

His 71 points in 88 playoff games are also the most in team history.

"It was a bumpy ride, for sure," Marchessault said. "A lot of hard work, especially the last few years."

There's also the sentimental aspect for these six.

They were part of the inaugural team who had to get to know the community before they played a game. In their first season in Las Vegas, they visited blood banks and first responders in a city still reeling from the Oct. 1, 2017 mass shooting that killed 58 people that night, and later 60.

Getting to the Stanley Cup Final in Year 1, though losing to the Washington Capitals, was storybook stuff.

The Golden Knights wasted no time celebrating after dominating the Panthers in Game 5 and capturing the first Stanley Cup in franchise history. (AP Images)

But the Golden Knights went into that final hoping to win more for the healing city as much, if not more, than for themselves.

To ultimately win it in front of a sold-out T-Mobile Arena made the moment even more special.

"It was redemption night, right?" Carrier said. "Put the boys out there, and it was emotional. We had business to do."

There are other names on this roster that will get their flowers.

Jack Eichel more than delivered in his first taste of playoff hockey with a league-best 26 points (six goals, 20 assists).

Goalie Adin Hill finished 11-4 after getting thrown into the fire in Game 3 of the second round against Edmonton with the exit of starting goaltender Laurent Brossoit. Hill ended up producing one of the best stretch runs by a goalie in recent memory — to the point that fans were chanting his name after every save.

Stone, off his second back surgery in less than a year, finished with 24 points (11 goals, 13 assists) in 22 games.

All are worthy of praise, and all will be recognized in due time. But they also know where it all began. The remaining six were part of the group that many felt would be the worst expansion team of all time. They were Cinderella then.

Every story needs a "happily ever after" moment. The Golden Knights now have theirs.

"We've been here for six years," Marchessault said. "We grinded. We wanted to get back and have that feeling we had the first year, to get back to the dance. We knew that this year, if we got back, things would be different. It was just fun to be a part of it." ∎

Golden Knights captain Mark Stone was the first player to raise the Stanley Cup after scoring a hat trick in the clinching Game 5 win. (Steve Marcus / Las Vegas Sun)

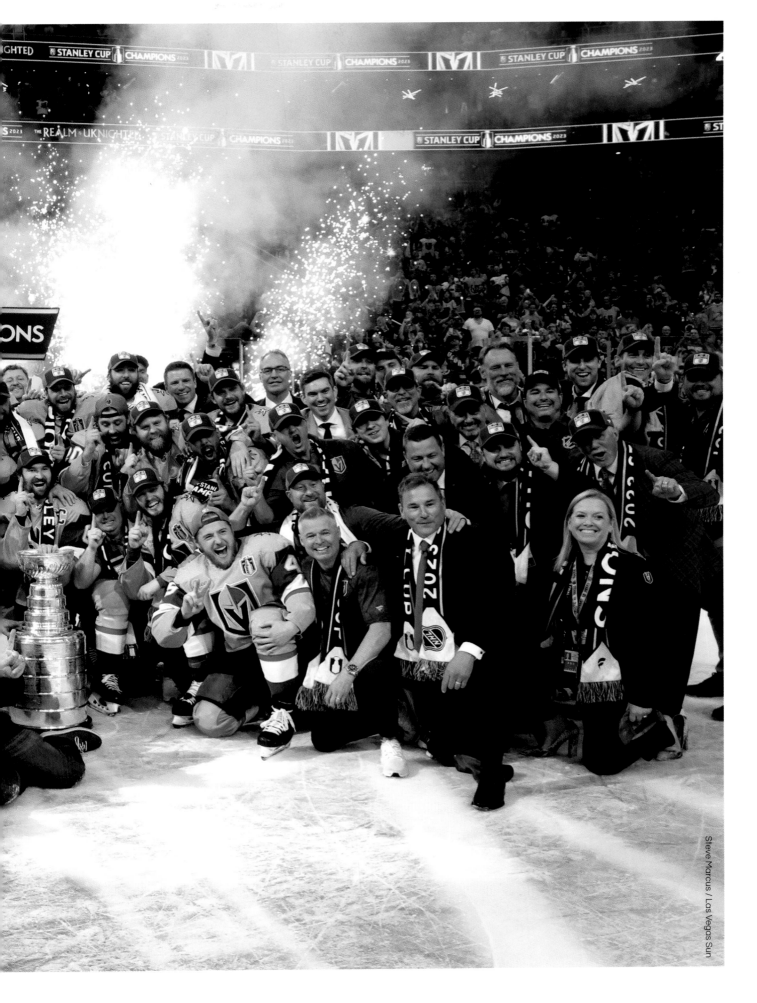

Steve Marcus / Las Vegas Sun

AP IMAGES

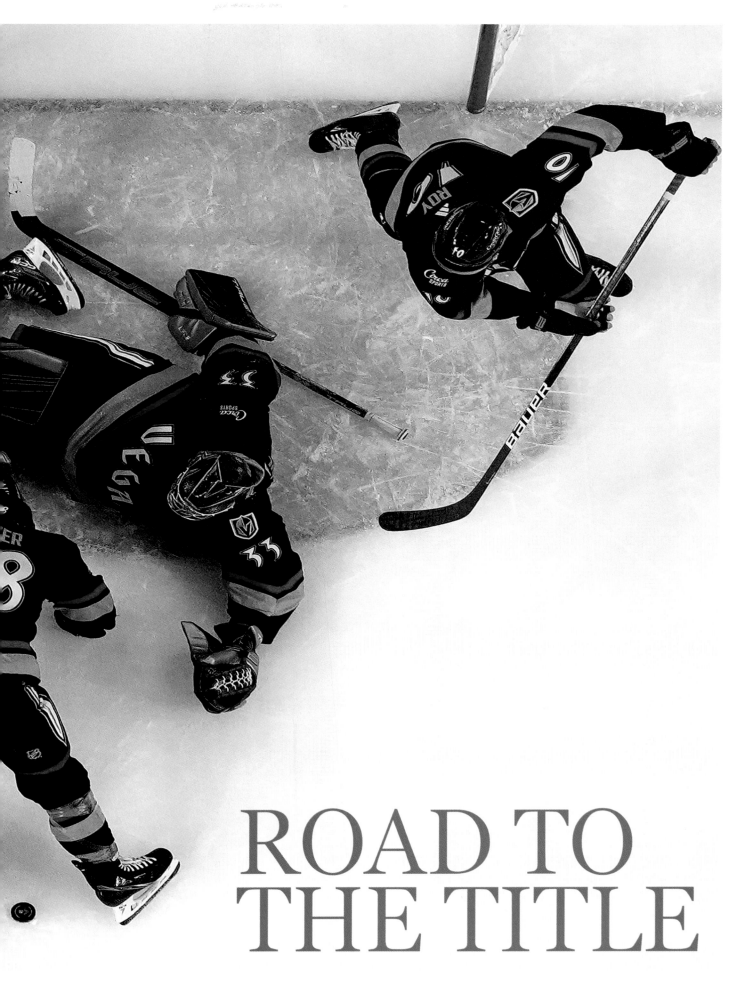

ROAD TO
THE TITLE

10 MOMENTS FROZEN IN TIME

Highlights from the Golden Knights' Road to the Stanley Cup Final

By Danny Webster • June 2, 2023

What a difference a year makes.

Last spring, the Vegas Golden Knights were watching the Stanley Cup playoffs from home for the first time.

They didn't have a coach.

Their No. 1 goalie and captain were both having surgery.

Whispers grew if this was the beginning of the end of their dominance as a top team after their first five seasons in the league.

What a bounce back season this has been. The Golden Knights recorded a franchise-record 111 points to clinch the top seed in the Western Conference, and eliminated the Winnipeg Jets, Edmonton Oilers and Dallas Stars to reach the Stanley Cup Final for the first time since that magical run in their inaugural 2017-18 season.

It's been quite the journey from the season opener to clinching a spot in the Final, and there have been plenty of moments to remember. We narrowed it down to these 10, in chronological order.

1: Oct. 11, 2022 at Los Angeles (4-3 win)

Five months after undergoing his first of what would be two back surgeries in less than a year, Mark Stone scored the game-winning goal with 24.9 seconds left. The Golden Knights' captain dealt with back issues on three occasions last season, the first being in the second game of the season in Los Angeles. This time around, the memories in Crypto.com Arena were more jovial.

2: Nov. 10, 2022 at Buffalo (7-4 win)

Jack Eichel's return to Buffalo didn't go so well. His second visit will long be remembered. The former Sabres captain, who was traded to Vegas in November 2021 for forwards Alex Tuch and Peyton Krebs, recorded a hat trick in the third period at KeyBank Center. One of the lasting images was after Eichel's first goal, extending his arms like actor Russell Crowe, asking the Buffalo crowd, "Are you not entertained?" That win also extended Vegas' winning streak to nine games, one shy of tying the team record.

One year after being traded to the Golden Knights, Jack Eichel scored a hat trick in Buffalo against his former team, the Sabres. (AP Images)

3: Dec. 5, 2022 at Boston (4-3 SO win)

Speaking of return games, Bruce Cassidy's first in Boston was also celebrated with a victory. Cassidy coached his first game against the Bruins after being fired by them last summer following six seasons and one Stanley Cup Final appearance — a loss in seven games to the St. Louis Blues in 2019. In this contest, the Golden Knights jumped out to a 3-0 lead behind two goals from rookie Paul Cotter before the Bruins rallied to force overtime. Vegas' Reilly Smith scored the lone goal by either team in the tiebreaker as the Golden Knights ended Boston's NHL-record winning streak for home victories to open a season at 14.

4: Dec. 31, 2022 vs. Nashville (5-4 OT win)

The New Year's Eve games at T-Mobile Arena have always had some memorable moments. This one nearly was for all the wrong reasons. Nashville's Filip Forsberg scored two of his three goals in the third period, including the tying goal with five seconds remaining in regulation. Vegas had to play the final 10 minutes and overtime with four defensemen — Brayden McNabb was ejected midway through the second period for fighting, and Daniil Miromanov left in the third after blocking a shot. Defenseman Nic Hague scored the winning goal at 2:04 of overtime — the first such tally of his career — to give the Golden Knights something to celebratewhile closing December with a 7-6-1 record.

5: Feb. 25 vs. Dallas (3-2 SO loss)

It has to be a crazy moment for it to be remembered in a loss. That's how goalie Laurent Brossoit's sequence was in overtime against the Stars. Dallas got a 2-on-1 early in the extra period. Jason Robertson's initial shot from the right side was saved. The rebound trickled to Tyler Seguin in the slot, and Brossoit barrel-rolled on his back to get a glove on Seguin's attempt. That was part of a 41-save evening for Brossoit in the journeyman's third NHL start after offseason hip surgery. He also made, arguably, the best save ever at T-Mobile Arena.

6. March 9 at Tampa Bay (4-3 OT win)

Injuries to Brossoit, Adin Hill and Logan Thompson forced the Golden Knights to add goalie insurance before the trade deadline. Enter longtime Vegas rival Jonathan Quick, who was acquired at the deadline from the Columbus Blue Jackets one day after being dealt by the Kings. Four days after making his Golden Knights debut, Quick had to face the Lightning, who were denied a third consecutive Stanley Cup last season, at Amalie Arena. Despite being severely outplayed through two periods, Vegas took a 3-1 lead midway through the third, only for Tampa's high-powered offense to force overtime. Alec Martinez scored at 3:09 of overtime to give Vegas its fourth win in five games. Quick finished with 34 saves that night and followed with a 33-save shutout in Carolina two nights later.

7: April 20 vs. Winnipeg; Round 1, Game 2 (5-2 win)

After losing 5-1 in Game 1, the Golden Knights answered in an emphatic way to tie the series in Game 2. Leading the way was Stone, who three months prior underwent his second back surgery and was in his second game back in the lineup. Stone scored twice in the third period to lead his team to a win. Vegas went on to win the next three, with the next moment coming days later.

Laurent Brossoit recorded 41 saves against the Dallas Stars in one of the most impressive goaltending performances of the season.

8: April 22 at Winnipeg; Round 1, Game 3 (5-4 2OT win)

The Golden Knights' depth has been a focal point in why they reached the Stanley Cup Final. Michael Amadio, who had a career-high 16 goals this season, scored 3:40 into the second extra frame — his first playoff winner after the Golden Knights squandered a 4-1 third-period lead. That game took the life out of the Jets. Vegas scored 18 goals in Games 2 through 5 after falling in Game 1.

9: May 14 at Edmonton; Round 2, Game 6 (5-2 win)

After going back and forth through the series and following a thrilling Game 5 win at T-Mobile Arena, the Golden Knights ended the Oilers' season with a come-from-behind effort for the ages. Jonathan Marchessault recorded a natural hat trick, and Adin Hill stopped 38 straight shots after allowing goals on the first two shots from the Oilers. William Karlsson and Reilly Smith also scored and Vegas put an end to the seasons of Edmonton's high-scoring duo of Connor McDavid and Leon Draisaitl.

10: May 29 at Dallas; Round 3, Game 6 (6-0 win)

The Golden Knights went into Game 6 trying for the third time to advance to the Stanley Cup Final. Stars coach — and former Vegas bench boss — Pete DeBoer even said the pressure shifted back to Vegas. The Golden Knights went on to play their best game of the playoffs, aided by a three-goal first period including the first of two scores by Karlsson, to move on Final. Hill, who is 7-3 in the playoffs since replacing the injured Brossoit in Game 3 against Edmonton, made 23 saves en route to his second shutout of the series. ■

William Karlsson celebrates with Michael Amadio after scoring a second goal in the decisive Game 6 of the Western Conference Final. (AP Images)

36
GOALTENDER

LOGAN THOMPSON

From Undrafted to NHL Starter, Thompson is One of the League's Best Stories

By Case Keefer | October 14, 2022

By his own admission, Logan Thompson was shaking from the nerves in his NHL debut.

It's hard to believe that was only 21 game appearances ago after watching the goalie in in the Vegas Golden Knights' home opener at T-Mobile Arena.

The 25-year-old was as staunch as a stone wall when pucks were flying at him and looked as self-assured as a long-time veteran the rest of the time he was on the ice during the 1-0 victory over the Chicago Blackhawks.

Thompson stopped 27 shots — the same number of saves he also registered in a 4-3 season-opening win at Los Angeles — for the second shutout of his career.

"He was excellent," Vegas coach Bruce Cassidy said in his post-game news conference. "He needed to be."

It's supposed to be the other way around for the Golden Knights this season: Their crew of star-studded skaters are supposed to make up for an unproven set of goaltenders. Just don't tell Thompson that.

Or maybe do tell him that, considering he's openly driven by the haters and "keyboard warriors" that have continually counted him out. A lot of

Logan Thompson started the 2022-23 season strong and became the first rookie goaltender named to the NHL All-Star Game since 2016. (AP Images)

athletes express a similar motivation, so often, in fact, that any statement in that vein should elicit eyerolls.

But Thompson is an exception. He's a player who's had everything stacked against him with few, if any, believers in his corner — and he's been through all that recently.

After making an impression in the one aforementioned appearance and a short stint with the team at the end of the 2020-2021 season, Thompson wasn't even seriously considered as a backup option for Robin Lehner going into last year. Vegas general manager Kelly McCrimmon surely didn't mean to denigrate Thompson back then, but it came off that way when he said he wanted to find an "NHL goalie" — eventually Laurent Brossoit — to be Lehner's understudy.

It was a return to the Henderson Silver Knights for Thompson, where he had already dominated with back-to-back Goalie of the Month awards upon first arriving. At least that was preferable to where the attendee of Brock University in St. Catherine's, Ontario, was two years prior when the NHL season began.

"I was in my one-bedroom college apartment eating pizza and drinking beer watching opening day," Thompson reminisced in the locker room after beating the Blackhawks.

He was now worlds away from that, admitting he never would have thought back then that his circumstances would change so drastically this quickly. Thompson received a roar from the sell-out crowd of 18,467 fans when he was announced as the starter pregame, and then gave them reasons to get even louder minutes later.

Thompson had the first highlight of the night when he turned away a shot from Andreas Athanasiou on a breakaway with a pad save. He then stopped a scoring chance from nine-time All-Star Patrick Kane.

The Golden Knights couldn't keep the Blackhawks out of their zone, however, and Thompson had to make his best save later in the first period. He was on his side but stacked his pads amid traffic to save a shot wristed his way.

"I think that was just a holy (expletive) moment," he said. "You see a guy winding up for a shot and you just hopefully get big and it hits you right. I couldn't get up, so luckily, it hit me."

Thompson said the early success helped him settle in, but he didn't have to do much the rest of the game. Even though Vegas never generated much offense, it bore down defensively and played much better in front of him in the second and third periods.

That's more along the lines of how the Golden Knights were expected to win this season in the wake of Lehner undergoing hip surgery that will keep him sidelined the whole year. That could be another case of selling Thompson short though, and by now, everyone should have learned their lesson in that regard.

Thompson proved doubters wrong at the end of last year when he nearly willed the Golden Knights to the playoffs when pressed into a starting role for 17 games at the end of the year because of Lehner's injury and Brossoit's ineffectiveness. And he's been even better so far this year.

He doesn't want to be seen as a liability or a weakness that the rest of the team needs to protect.

"We're not going to be able to put up four goals every night," Thompson said.

Thompson might be relatively new to all this, but he's shown he's more than capable of rising to the occasion. He's no longer scared of his moment in the NHL.

"He's got a lot of confidence in himself," forward Reilly Smith said. "He's come into camp and wanted to prove himself to everyone. He's a talented goalie and I think he's going to keep on taking steps forward." ∎

Logan Thompson's promising season was cut short due to a lower-body injury in February. The Golden Knights started five goalies in 2022-23, deftly navigating injuries while pursuing their first Stanley Cup. (AP Images)

PAST IS PROLOGUE

Golden Knights Hang On to Beat Bruins as Cassidy makes First Return to Boston

By Danny Webster • December 5, 2022

Bruce Cassidy wasn't sure he'd even get a video tribute. He wasn't going to hold it against his former team if they didn't.

As the video played on the TD Garden jumbotron, the camera cut back to the former Boston Bruins coach with tears evident down his face.

The Golden Knights wanted this one for their new coach, and it took a five-round shootout to get it done. Reilly Smith scored the lone goal in the extra frame to secure a 4-3 shootout victory for Vegas in Cassidy's first game against his former team.

Cassidy was presented with a tribute video in the first period to highlight the coach's six years with the Bruins. He led Boston to the playoffs in all six seasons, including a trip to the Stanley Cup Final in 2019, before he was fired in June.

This time, Cassidy will leave Boston with his new group ending the Bruins' franchise-record 14-game home winning streak to begin the season.

"That's something I'll get choked up about in about three seconds," Cassidy said. "I appreciate it. It's that simple. I appreciate it."

Cassidy knew this game was coming. It was something he wanted to get over with as soon as possible. The fact that his new team — now 19-7-1 and atop the Western Conference — was facing his old team at a league-best 20 wins made storylines simple.

"The streak was irrelevant for me," Cassidy said. "It was just nice to come in and play well tonight."

But the Golden Knights closed this four-game road trip with three wins and were one third-period collapse in Pittsburgh away from sweeping it.

Much like those other games, this one wouldn't be easy.

Paul Cotter started the first two-goal game of his career 1:36 into the first period with a one-timer from the left circle. Cotter, who was bumped to the top line in place of the injured Jack Eichel (lower body), scored for the first time since Nov. 10.

"It was great to get that win," Cotter said. "A big statement for us."

Jonathan Marchessault doubled the lead less than four minutes later after forcing a turnover and beating Boston goalie Jeremy Swayman with his own rebound.

Cotter scored again 51 seconds into the second period to give the Golden Knights a 3-0 lead. All four times during this road trip the Golden Knights led 2-0, and they blew the lead each time.

Bruce Cassidy acknowledges applause while being honored in a video tribute for his previous career as head coach of the Boston Bruins. (AP Images)

Knowing the firepower that Boston has, there wasn't any shock from Cassidy's point of view.

Brad Marchand got the Bruins on the board midway through the second period on a deflection, and David Pastrnak cut it to 3-2 with 36 seconds left in the frame.

It was a matter of time before the Bruins took over the game, and they did so in the final 40 minutes, outshooting Vegas 29-15.

But that was a reflection of how good Logan Thompson was yet again.

Thompson made 40 saves, one start after making a career-high 43 in the recent 4-3 loss in Pittsburgh. Six of those saves came in overtime and a bulk came during a 4-on-3 power play in the final minutes.

Even when Taylor Hall tied it 3-3 at 3:08 of the third period, Thompson stood tall and made key saves on the penalty kill. Boston's only power-play goal out of four chances came as a 5-on-3 penalty expired, with Hall scoring shortly after.

"They're at home. We knew they were going to push back," Cotter said. "We know our game. We went up early for a reason."

After winning a seven-round shootout one week ago in Columbus to preserve a victory at the start of this road trip, Thompson stopped all five Boston attempts to push the Golden Knights to a league-best 12-2-1 on the road.

The win is more impressive knowing the Golden Knights won without Eichel and defenseman Alex Pietrangelo, two of their top scorers. Eichel is listed as day-to-day, while Pietrangelo missed his fourth straight game due to personal reasons.

Maybe it was wanting to win for Cassidy. Maybe it was the money Cassidy put on the board — a tradition in NHL locker rooms that money is put on the line when a former player or coach faces his former team. Cassidy wouldn't say how much it was, but it was important enough to leave a dent.

"Cassidy college fund went down a little bit," he said.

But Cassidy admitted it was good to get this one over with. He said he's grateful for his time in Boston and while it might not have resulted in a championship, the foundation he helped create has put Boston in a good place going forward.

Cassidy added he wouldn't mind being back in Boston during the spring. Specifically, May or June.

"Tonight, it showed that we wanted to play for a guy like that," Marchessault said. "He's been great for us since he got here." ∎

The Golden Knights were quick to rally behind new head coach Bruce Cassidy after his arrival from Boston. (Steve Marcus / Las Vegas Sun)

GOLDEN MISFITS

Remaining Original Golden Knights Prepare for Another Playoff Run

By Danny Webster • April 13, 2023

Six players remain from the beloved Golden Knights team that improbably advanced to the Stanley Cup Finals in its inaugural season. Call them the pillars of the franchise, a foundation that has stayed strong enough to help deliver Vegas to the Playoffs in five of its six seasons.

William Karlsson, Jonathan Marchessault, Reilly Smith, William Carrier, Brayden McNabb and Shea Theodore have stayed the course in Vegas since 2018, despite roster turnover elsewhere. They're now being rewarded with another golden opportunity to match the initial magical run, if not top it.

The Western Conference has looked wide open all season, giving the Golden Knights a clear path back to the Stanley Cup Final.

"It's not something you can take for granted," Marchessault says of the near-perennial success. "For me, I've been pretty lucky. I didn't make the playoffs two years of my 11, 12-year career. I consider myself lucky."

One of his non-playoff years came last season. Having suffered injuries galore, the Golden Knights fought to stay alive until the penultimate game of their regular season, when they were officially eliminated. They did so without stars Mark Stone and Max

Pacioretty for half of the season, and other standouts like Karlsson and Alec Martinez, to name a few, also missed significant time.

Injuries have struck again this season, and though they haven't hit quite as hard, they might again be the biggest hurdle standing in the way of a long playoff run. Carrier has a lower-body injury that has him out indefinitely, while Theodore's playoff status is also up in the air with the same designation.

In addition, Stone has been out since January and underwent back surgery. He recently began light skating as part of his rehab, and though he could possibly return at some point, it likely won't be early in the playoffs.

Goaltending is something of question mark, too. Logan Thompson and Adin Hill appear close to returning after dealing with lower-body injuries that sidelined them and dampened what had been strong play for stretches throughout the season. But there's no guarantee either of them will see postseason action if Laurent Brossoit takes control of the goaltending job by continuing the high level of play he locked into late in the regular season.

"Opportunities like this don't come every year," Marchessault says of the playoffs. "You have to be in

Right wing Reilly Smith carries the puck against the Edmonton Oilers during Game 2 of their second-round playoff series. Smith was one of six members of the Golden Knights' inaugural roster who led the team to a Stanley Cup in the franchise's sixth NHL season. (Steve Marcus / Las Vegas Sun)

the moment, take it one game at a time and take care of business."

Marchessault, Karlsson and Smith—the trio forever known as "the Misfit Line"—have certainly taken care of their end this season. Although they haven't stayed on the same line together as in the past, their production has remained high.

Marchessault led the team with 28 regular-season goals, and his 57 points placed him behind only Jack Eichel and Chandler Stephenson.

Injuries thwarted Smith's chances at his first career 30-goal season, but he has still exceeded expectations in the first year of a three-year, $15 million extension signed on the first day of free agency last July.

Karlsson, meanwhile, has made the biggest leap of the three. After seeing his play decline from his 43-goal expansion season, he has rebounded for his first 50-point campaign since 2018-2019 and amassed a career-high 39 assists.

Those three original Misfits have kept the team humming throughout the franchise's existence. Even on a star-studded roster headlined by the likes of Eichel and Alex Pietrangelo, those in the Vegas locker room point to Marchessault, Karlsson and Smith as the engine of the team.

Nothing might ever match what they achieved their first year in Vegas, when Karlsson was scoring highlight-reel goals and the line was converting odd-man rushes with ease, but the experience has proven beneficial for them.

"That was the best hockey anyone in that lineup played in their life," Marchessault says about the expansion year. "That's something that's never going to be repeated."

Entering the 2023 postseason, Smith is the team's all-time leader in playoff points with 52, while Marchessault leads Vegas with 21 playoff goals. Marchessault became a local legend during the 2018 playoff run, when he scored 21 points in 20 games.

"Even still, to this day, I'm chasing the playoffs I had [that year]," Marchessault says. "I want to get better. I'm still looking to get better."

While this might not be the most talented team the Golden Knights have put on the ice—the 2020-2021 team that led the league in points at the time of the COVID-19 season interruption is tough to top in that department—this year's group is still well-equipped to compete against any opponent. And, once again, it's largely on the backs of those who started it all.

"They care about the Golden Knights' legacy," coach Bruce Cassidy says. "They're original guys, and they want to be remembered for that. I think they take a lot of pride in that. I see it in their work every day, staying in the lineup, by being healthy, taking care of themselves." ■

Center William Karlsson rebounded during the 2022-23 season, recording 53 points and 39 assists in the regular season. (Steve Marcus / Las Vegas Sun)

9

FORWARD

JACK EICHEL

Entering His First Playoff Run, Eichel Sheds Past Labels

By Danny Webster | April 18, 2023

Jack Eichel might have the most important role in the Golden Knights' locker room.

It's a power Eichel wields that if one wrong decision is made, it could cause an uproar among his teammates. If a choice doesn't sit well with them, there might be a side eye or two his way.

Such is the life of the team DJ.

Requests will come Eichel's way on what songs are played to get the day going — whether it's following a morning skate or after a gym session at City National Arena. Eichel, normally in control of the iPad, sets the tone.

"Some days I'm an indie rock guy, some days I like hip-hop, some days some tropical chill," said the Golden Knights' star center. "I can go all over the place. It depends on what the mood calls for."

Though Eichel will say it's a shared responsibility — defenseman Shea Theodore handles the tunes on gameday — it's usually his call. But he enjoys "what other people like to listen to, so I can judge them."

This season, Eichel gets to do something he's never done — handle the team's Spotify account for a playoff run.

Eichel, 26, will play in the Stanley Cup Playoffs for the first time in his career when the Golden Knights open the first round against the visiting Winnipeg Jets as the No. 1 seed in the Western Conference.

It's taken eight years for Eichel to compete for the Stanley Cup.

The first six seasons were spent with the Buffalo Sabres as a captain and perceived savior for a franchise that hoped for a return to glory. Following

Jack Eichel passes among a host of Winnipeg Jets players during the Golden Knights first-round playoff series. (Steve Marcus / Las Vegas Sun)

disappointing campaigns — and a neck surgery conundrum that soured both sides — Eichel was dealt to Vegas in November 2021.

Eichel was thrown into the fire fresh off an artificial disc replacement procedure that had never been done on an NHL player and is not believed to have been performed on a player in MLB, the NFL or the NBA to that point. A traditional disc replacement would have likely sidelined him for the entire season.

He returned much sooner than expected, missing about three months, and tallied 14 goals with 11 assists in 34 games. But despite Eichel's efforts, the Golden Knights were eliminated from postseason contention for the first time after falling to the Chicago Blackhawks in a shootout in the second to last game of the season.

In 2022-23, Vegas rebounded to win its third Pacific Division title and clinch home-ice advantage. Eichel posted a team-high 66 points (27 goals, 39 assists) in 67 games.

"I'm excited about it. It's something I've waited for a while, and it's something the group has worked really hard to grab this year," Eichel said. "I think after the way last year went, we all had a good focus coming into this season that we wanted to get back to the postseason and prove a lot of people wrong."

When Eichel arrived in Vegas, the "locker room cancer" label was thrown his way. Why couldn't a player of his talent, taken No. 2 overall after Connor McDavid went to the Edmonton Oilers in 2015, not find a way to will Buffalo to the playoffs? Was it him? Was he more selfish than selfless because of his neck issue? Was it the franchise not putting the right pieces around him, or was his presence just not suited to be on a championship contender?

The outside noise that came with Eichel never reached his new teammates.

Giving a glimpse

From the day Eichel took the ice for the first time with the Golden Knights in 2022, he had this business-like approach. He admitted last year, at times, that he put pressure on himself in a new situation to perform right away, to prove he was capable of being better than ever.

Last summer, people got a glimpse of Eichel's true personality. Eichel hit a home run during teammate Reilly Smith's annual charity softball game. Rounding the bases, Eichel nonchalantly cartwheeled across home plate to the shock and laughter of his teammates.

It was the first time Eichel looked comfortable in his new surroundings and showed off the kind of character he was.

"He's awesome," said center Chandler Stephenson, who has been linemates with Eichel for the majority of his time in Vegas. "He's always inclusive. He always wants to get together, go to dinner, always keeping it light. Doesn't take the game too seriously. Just has fun.

"He's obviously helped our team with the type of player that he is, but you could see the first week he was here, he opened up right away and he's a genuine dude."

Eichel took it a step further on March 1 when the Golden Knights introduced their season-long postgame tradition, where the player of the game dons an Elvis Presley wig and glasses. Eichel was given that honor after scoring twice in Vegas' 3-2 win over the Carolina Hurricanes.

Off the ice, Eichel opens his house nearly every day to his teammates. Whether it's to relax at the pool or play cards — 13 Up is the game of choice — Eichel has become that perfect combination of leader and teammate in the eyes of the locker room.

"He cares about everyone," defenseman Ben Hutton said. "He keeps it light on practice days, making jokes with everyone involved. At the same time, he's very competitive. He wants to win. He doesn't take it out on anyone. He's the hardest on himself."

Challenge issued

Bruce Cassidy challenged Eichel to take that next leap.

Already one of the more gifted offensive players in the league, Eichel was never seen as a defensive option.

Being the top-line center on a Cassidy-coached team comes with that responsibility at both ends of the ice.

Eichel had the best defensive season of his career this year, recording a plus-26 rating at 5-on-5 and a career-high 46 takeaways.

"I'm not surprised. He's been arguably our best defensive forward in terms of closing in our end, being on time, killing plays," Cassidy said. "I just think he's bought in with what we're trying to get him to do."

Eichel missed 15 games this season due to different lower-body injuries, and also took a puck to the face. There was a nine-game stretch before the All-Star break where Eichel had just one point in nine games.

Other than that, he's been the Golden Knights' most consistent offensive player.

Eichel's speed remains the best offensive threat Vegas has, both at 5-on-5 and on the power play. His ability to extend plays and use his long stick and reach separate him from the rest on the roster.

"He's one of those players who's just gifted," forward and linemate Jonathan Marchessault said. "He can turn it on whenever he wants. Especially when he's full speed, that's when he can create."

That added responsibility for Eichel had to come in handy once captain Mark Stone had his second back surgery in January and missed the second half of the regular season. Eichel was hit the most by Stone's absence, not having the two-time Selke Trophy finalist on his line.

Having bought into the 200-foot game allowed the rest of the forward group to follow suit. That's one of the reasons why Vegas went 22-4-5 since the All-Star break.

Eichel has been the biggest reason for that with 12 goals and 20 assists in 29 games in that stretch.

"We came into this season with something to prove," Eichel said. "I'm sure everyone wanted to prove something to the league, but we wanted to prove something to ourselves. I think we wanted to make a statement that last year was a bit of a fluke."

The next chapter

Eichel's love for music knows no bounds. He's always been a classic rock fan, growing up in a household where the Rolling Stones and The Beatles were sacred. Marvin Gaye and Van Morrison have always been favorites of his.

His go-to for music right now is Australian group Tame Impala, whose latest album "The Slow Rush" can best be described as psychedelic light rock with a hip-hop vibe.

One song on that album that might fit Eichel best is "On Track." The first verse reads, "Strictly speaking I'm holding on, more than a minor setback, but strictly speaking I'm still on track, and all of my dreams are still in sight, because strictly speaking I've got my whole life."

Eichel tasting playoff success for the first time is the next chapter in his life, that being his NHL career. It didn't seem bright after last year, knowing he missed the playoffs again. Things looked bleak. Maybe he was the cancer social media dictated him to be.

The duties of bringing a Stanley Cup to Las Vegas will rest on Eichel's shoulders. It's the responsibility he once faced as captain of the Sabres, and now as the star on the Golden Knights. He's also about to enter an unknown that he's never experienced with playoff hockey. This is the time of year when the superstars are evaluated higher than ever.

There have been many minor, and major, setbacks for Eichel. Right now, he's on track. It's on him to not veer off it.

"It was our goal this year at the start to get into the postseason. Good on us for getting there," Eichel said. "Now we've just got to finish the job here and continue to work toward that ultimate goal." ■

FALSE START

Self-Inflicted Mistakes Had Golden Knights Reeling in Game 1 Loss

By Danny Webster

While the Winnipeg Jets had to play close-to-perfect hockey down the stretch just to make the playoffs, the Golden Knights still played their share of meaningful games in the final weeks of the regular season.

That's why this result is a shocker.

It's not just that the Jets came into T-Mobile Arena and dominated the Golden Knights 5-1 in Game 1 of their first-round series. It's that the Jets stole home-ice advantage all-world goalie Connor Hellebuyck barely seeing any action, and the Golden Knights looking out of sorts for the majority of the night.

"We didn't play as confident," center Jack Eichel said, "and it just wasn't our best."

For the first playoff game at T-Mobile Arena since May 2021, the atmosphere was as some would remember. A raucous crowd of 18,006 had their rally towels at the ready, the volume was turned up to 10 and the excitement of being one of the last 16 teams remaining was evident.

But the best fight from the Golden Knights in Game 1 was from their pregame show when a golden dragon burned a projected jet to a crisp.

The Golden Knights were uncharacteristic aggressors early on. For a team that averaged 23 hits per game during the regular season, they had 27 in the first 20 minutes.

That was Vegas' best shot. Winnipeg answered with a haymaker.

The Jets scored twice in a 62-second span early in the second period thanks to their top line. Kyle Connor scored on a one-timer from center Pierre-Luc Dubois at 1:24 to open the scoring, then Dubois scored off a turnover for the 2-0 lead.

For Winnipeg to give Hellebuyck, arguably the best goalie in the world, that lead while already controlling the neutral zone and preventing easy entries was all it needed to stifle Vegas.

The Golden Knights got on the board late in the second when William Karlsson scored off the rush at 15:49 to cut the lead in half and reignite life into the home crowd.

Yet that was all Vegas could get. Winnipeg added three more in the third, including the eventual game-winner from Blake Wheeler 3:53 into the third for a 3-1 lead.

Two of those goals came off turnovers. One was off losing an offensive-zone faceoff.

"Those guys, especially that top line, they have high-end skill," captain Mark Stone said. "If you're going to turn it over, they're going to make you pay."

Part of that excitement was supposed to stem off the return of Stone, who was in the lineup for the first time since Jan. 12 after having his second back surgery in less than a year.

Stone, who started on the third line and was moved to the first line with Vegas looking for a spark, played 21:28 and was a minus-3.

"It felt like I had missed three months," Stone said. "Pace of the game is ramped up at this time (of year). Hopefully, just feel better going into next game, but no excuses. I've been in this league long enough to know what needs to be done."

Stone will wear the blame, but it was a game to forget for a lot of the star players.

Eichel had just two shots on goal in his first-ever playoff game. Five forwards — Jonathan Marchessault, Ivan Barbashev, Chandler Stephenson, Keegan Kolesar and Stone — did not have a single shot on goal. Winnipeg out-attempted Vegas 61-47.

Laurent Brossoit finished with 26 saves in his first playoff start against his former team and allowed four goals. It was far from his fault. Winnipeg had 14 shots in the first period and while Brossoit had shaky moments behind his net at times, he still turned away all shots in the first.

"It's playoff hockey," coach Bruce Cassidy said. "You need an intensity level that's greater than the one we had."

Cassidy switched the lines midway through the second and it lit a spark. Stone and Stephenson were moved to the top line with Eichel, while Marchessault, Karlsson and Smith were reunited. Marchessault assisted Karlsson on his goal.

But the rare opportunity off the rush was the only bright spot offensively that the Golden Knights produced in the final 40 minutes.

Vegas had two shots combined in the third period. Part of it was due to Winnipeg shutting down the neutral zone, but it was a microcosm of how off the Golden Knights were all night.

"Overall, not a great effort for us offensively," Stone said. "Defensively, it wasn't terrible. Most of the stuff they got was from bad offensive play."

If the Golden Knights can rest easy on anything, they weren't the only home team to lose Game 1. In fact, all four road teams in the West won their opening games with Colorado, Dallas and Edmonton all losing to start the playoffs.

Vegas has been in this situation as recently as the shortened season in 2021, when they lost Game 1 to Minnesota and Colorado in Rounds 1 and 2, respectively, before rallying to win both series.

Another effort like this could result in trouble for the top seed in the West, but the Golden Knights are confident in their ability to bounce back.

"I look at it now, we've got to win four out of six. It doesn't matter how you do it. You just got to do it," Stone said. "We'll have to just look at ourselves in the mirror and get it done." ■

BACK TO BASICS

Golden Knights Need to Keep Relying on 'Little Things' Against Winnipeg

By Danny Webster

The second period of Game 2 was more about the Golden Knights finding their game.

It didn't happen right away. It was a gradual crescendo following four periods of frustration, looking overmatched against the Winnipeg Jets and staring at a 2-0 series deficit if things didn't change quickly.

What changed?

"It's the little things," center William Karlsson said.

Keeping things simple has been the turn of phrase used by the Golden Knights following their disappointing effort in Game 1.

They tried to be the aggressor and hit everything that moved. Didn't work. They kept going for the big play, trying stretch passes from the defensive zone to spring breakaway opportunities at every opportunity. Didn't work.

After an emotional first period where the game nearly got away from Vegas, they started to dial it back. The little things Karlsson refers to showed up, and the Golden Knights carried that momentum for the final 35 minutes of the game to win 5-2 and even the best-of-7 series at a game apiece.

With the series shifting to Winnipeg for Game 3, that attention to detail will need to be sharpened heading into one of the loudest playoff environments in the NHL.

"Just keep doing the same things that made us successful after the first period," defenseman Zach Whitecloud said. "We did a good job both games starting the right way."

Whitecloud added the Jets got to their game first in both contests, and that's what swayed the pendulum in Winnipeg's favor early. In Game 1, Winnipeg answered Vegas' aggression with two goals in 62 seconds during the second period and secured all momentum.

Game 2 was much different with the Jets outshooting the Golden Knights 11-2 in the first 10-plus minutes, including the game's first goal from Winnipeg's Adam Lowry.

Frustration mounted late in the first when Pietrangelo and teammate Nicolas Roy were assessed roughing minors 15 seconds apart, leading to a 4-on-3 for the Jets and a chance to put the game away early.

The Jets had just one shot on goal in those two minutes. Little things.

"I think that was a bit of a momentum swing," Karlsson said. "Every time you can kill off a PK, especially a 4-on-3, I think that's going to give off a lot of energy."

Mark Stone celebrates his second goal in Game 2 as the Golden Knights bounced back from a loss in the series opener. (Steve Marcus / Las Vegas Sun)

> ## "When you win puck battles, everything opens up, right?" Karlsson said. "We get puck movement, we get people at the net and good things happen."
> — Center William Karlsson

That translated to the second period in question.

Karlsson deserves an abundance of credit for being the lone driver of offense through a game-and-a-half, but his goal in Game 2 was a byproduct of extending pressure in the offensive zone and winning puck battles. The sustained offensive zone pressure eventually led to Karlsson gathering the loose puck and firing it over Connor Hellebuyck's glove to tie the game.

Little things.

"When you win puck battles, everything opens up, right?" Karlsson said. "We get puck movement, we get people at the net and good things happen."

The same can be said for Jack Eichel's goal five minutes later that gave the Golden Knights their first lead of the series. After an offensive-zone faceoff, Jonathan Marchessault and Michael Amadio worked behind the net to maintain possession, found Pietrangelo for the shot that was tipped by Eichel for the 2-1 advantage.

Coach Bruce Cassidy said that goal is one the Golden Knights can build off of and use it as an example of how to score in the playoffs with teams protecting the crease more than usual.

"It's a good hockey goal for us because we're below the goal line against their D, which was part of our gameplan, is make them work down low," Cassidy said. "Amadio and Marchy did a really good job. They separated down low, they held on to pucks."

Little things.

By the time the Jets tied it 2-2 late in the second, those goals already dictated the pace for the third. The Golden Knights continued the game plan of putting pucks behind the Winnipeg net and winning battles to set up plays in the offensive zone.

That needs to continue if the Golden Knights want to reclaim home-ice advantage. They put 39 shots on Hellebuyck after just 17 in Game 1. Vegas had 12 high-danger chances — eight of them in the final two periods — and outshot Winnipeg 31-16 in the final 40 minutes after the Jets had a 17-8 edge in the first.

Perhaps that's why the road to 16 wins is a marathon. It's the little things along the way that can help get the Golden Knights there.

"We feel we have a very good hockey team," Eichel said. "I don't think we played to our standard in Game 1. It was important for us to get back to what makes us successful as a team in Game 2, and we did that." ∎

Officials break up fights during an aggressive first period of Game 2. The Golden Knights found their stride in the second period and carried that momentum throughout the series. (Steve Marcus / Las Vegas Sun)

✦ WESTERN CONFERENCE FIRST ROUND GAME 3 ✦
April 22, 2023 • Winnipeg, Saskatchewan
Golden Knights 5, Jets 4 (2OT)

'WE GRINDED ALL NIGHT FOR THAT ONE'

Amadio Caps Off 2OT Road Thriller as Golden Knights Lead Series

By Danny Webster

Michael Amadio's soft-spoken manner doesn't allow for many moments where he can express exuberant joy. Scoring his first postseason goal — and having it be the game-winner — is one way to reach that apex.

Amadio, who scored a career-high 16 goals during the regular season, found the back of the net 3:40 into the second overtime as the Golden Knights overcame a third-period rally by the Winnipeg Jets for a nail-biting 5-4 win at Canada Life Centre.

Shortly after a Vegas power play expired, a makeshift line of Amadio, Ivan Barbashev and Brett Howden took the ice. A clearing attempt by Jets defenseman Dylan Samberg deflected off Barbashev's skate to Amadio, who turned in the slot and beat Connor Hellebuyck.

"It was a pretty special feeling," said Amadio, who added he didn't even know he scored until he turned back to see his teammates mob him. "We grinded all night for that one."

What may go down as one of the more exciting playoff games in Golden Knights history was almost remembered for all the wrong reasons. Vegas carried a 4-1 lead into the third period after it controlled play throughout.

The Golden Knights got there thanks to two goals from Jack Eichel and goals from Chandler Stephenson and Keegan Kolesar. Eichel added an assist for his first three-point playoff game and four over the last two contests. Stephenson had an assist for his second straight multipoint game.

But the Jets, who already overachieved by stealing Game 1 on the road against the top seed in the Western Conference, rallied behind their roaring home crowd and the intimidating Winnipeg Whiteout to make a run.

Nino Niederreiter scored 2:04 into the third period to make it 4-2, followed by Mark Scheifele's power-play goal at 14:08 with Phil Kessel serving a holding minor. With Hellebuyck pulled for an extra skater, Adam Lowry scored his fourth goal of the series with 21.9 seconds remaining to force extra time.

Michael Amadio, Alec Martinez, Brett Howden and Ivan Barbashev celebrate Amadio's goal in the second overtime against the Winnipeg Jets in Game 3. (AP Images)

"We kind of regrouped going back (into the locker room) for overtime," Amadio said. "We know what we had in this room."

The Jets managed to rally despite Norris Trophy-contending defenseman Josh Morrissey leaving the game due to a lower-body injury in his second shift of the matchup. Jets coach Rick Bowness said Morrissey (16 goals and 60 assists this season, both career highs) will not play the remainder of the series.

Yet playing with five defensemen including Neal Pionk, who drew three assists in the third-period rally and logged a game-high 41:08, the Jets nearly had a comeback to remember before running out of steam.

"I didn't feel like we were in trouble," Golden Knights coach Bruce Cassidy said. "We have a veteran group. Two things go into that. You shouldn't give up a lead when you have a veteran group. You should find a way to get it to the finish line. We also have a veteran group who can put it behind us."

The Golden Knights were one of the best road teams in the league this season with a 26-7-8 mark. Cassidy said that he felt the effort all year away from T-Mobile Arena could transfer to the postseason.

It didn't take long for that to hold true. Kolesar and Jets defenseman Brenden Dillon dropped the gloves 49 seconds into the game, carrying over the intensity from a physical Game 2.

Just like Game 1, the Golden Knights channeled that energy in their favor. Stephenson opened the scoring 2:52 into the game off an assist from Mark Stone.

Stephenson found Eichel for a one-timer with the man advantage and a 2-0 lead less than four minutes later.

Kyle Connor, Winnipeg's top scorer this season with 80 points, made it 2-1 on a deflection at 9:07, but the Golden Knights kept the Jets at bay offensively through two periods. Vegas outshot Winnipeg 26-11 over the first 40 minutes and had a 47-33 edge in shot attempts in all situations.

Vegas added with two more goals in the second period. Eichel scored his second at 10:46 on another one-timer on the power play, followed by Kolesar at 17:45.

"It's hard to win hockey games in the playoffs and we'll take them however we can get them," Stone said. "We want to close that game out for sure, right? They played five defense all night. We kept putting pucks behind them, rolled four lines, three D-pairs, and we found a way."

If there was any worry that the Golden Knights wouldn't carry their play from the last two periods in Game 2 over to Game 3, they were quickly erased. Even the power play, which was heavily maligned following Game 1, found a way to score twice. When the second-period buzzer sounded, the Golden Knights had outscored the Jets 9-2 over the previous four periods.

The moment defining that dominance came after Kolesar's goal to make it 4-1. As he slammed his hands into the glass to celebrate, TV cameras caught a Jets fan staring back at Kolesar, arms outreached, nodding his way in an odd form of intimidation.

Playoff hockey, however, provided one subtle reminder: One bad period can easily wipe out a dominant 40 minutes. The Golden Knights were one goal away from what would've been another memorable playoff collapse. Cue all memories from Game 7 against the San Jose Sharks in 2019.

But Vegas has found a way, after things went haywire in Game 1, to steal back home-ice advantage. Suddenly, the Golden Knights can put the pressure on with a win in Game 4.

Such is the roller coaster that is playoff hockey.

"We won't be the first team to let a lead slip away," Cassidy said. "We've been through it a little bit this year. We're an imperfect team, but we tend to find a way to bounce back." ∎

Keegan Kolesar, Jack Eichel and Michael Amadio celebrate Kolesar's goal past Winnipeg Jets goaltender Connor Hellebuyck during the second period. (AP Images)

LOUD AND CLEAR

Brossoit Silences Jets, Crowd in 4-2 Win

By Danny Webster

Laurent Brossoit heard it loud and clear. It didn't faze him.

Because once upon a time, yes, he was a backup. But this backup is one win from advancing to the second round of the Stanley Cup Playoffs and sending his former team home for the summer.

Brossoit made 24 saves, including some key saves in the second period, to help push the Golden Knights to a 4-2 win over the Winnipeg Jets in Game 4 of their first-round series and take a commanding 3-1 series lead.

Brossoit, the former Winnipeg goalie who backed up Connor Hellebuyck for three seasons, was met with chants of "You're a backup!" throughout the course of the night. At times against his former team he had looked like one, with 10 goals allowed through three games.

But in a must-win game to seize control of the series, Brossoit bested Hellebuyck.

"Oh, yeah. I heard it," Brossoit said. "It's fuel."

Brett Howden scored the first two playoff goals of his career — and recorded his first two-goal game in the NHL — and William Karlsson scored for the third time this series to help the Golden Knights come within one win of their seventh series victory since entering the league in 2017-18.

Vegas is 3-0 all-time when leading a series 3-1 with home-ice advantage.

"He was ready from the get-go," defenseman Shea Theodore said of Brossoit. "We know how well we can play. It didn't seem like much fazed him."

In a unique set of circumstances, the pressure was on in Game 4 even more than for Game 3 for the Golden Knights. They stole back home-ice advantage, but they knew going into Monday that the Jets would attempt to bounce back after losing the 5-4 double overtime thriller Saturday.

Vegas got Winnipeg's best punch to start when Blake Wheeler scored a power-play goal at 5:53 of the first to open the scoring and give the Jets the lead.

But the Jets had to play a majority of the game without one of their key players for the second straight contest when forward Mark Scheifele suffered an upper-body injury after his breakaway attempt was stopped by Brossoit. Scheifele's momentum led him shoulder first into the boards.

Winnipeg was already without top defenseman Josh Morrissey (lower body), who is out for the rest of the series. Jets coach Rick Bowness has not ruled out Scheifele.

Despite the Jets scoring the first goal, the Golden

Laurent Brossoit makes a save against the Winnipeg Jets' Mark Scheifele during the first period. Brossoit ignored the chants from fans of his former team and made 24 saves in the 4-2 win. (AP Images)

Knights once again found an answer. The thoughts of struggling to find their footing in Game 1 and looking outmatched appear to be a distant memory.

The catalyst on this night was Howden. His promotion in the lineup to play with Chandler Stephenson and Mark Stone has highlighted Howden's effectiveness this series. Coach Bruce Cassidy said at morning skate that Howden's speed has been an effective weapon at both ends of the ice.

That was on display four minutes after Wheeler's goal. Howden forced a turnover at the Winnipeg blue line to kickstart a 3-on-2. Howden received a pass from Stephenson, his first shot attempt was blocked, but he followed through on the rebound to tie it 1-1.

The good news for the Jets is their power play was still efficient without Scheifele and Morrissey. Winnipeg scored on both of its attempts and has scored three straight 5-on-4 goals.

Even strength has been the difference. Bowness confirmed as much, saying that both teams are getting their chances at 5-on-5.

"Pucks are going in for them, and they aren't for us," Bowness said. "We need to find more of those greasy ones."

Both of Vegas' goals in the second period were of the "greasy" variety.

Karlsson gave the Golden Knights the lead at 13:32 as a power play expired, when the shot from Jonathan Marchessault deflected off his skate. Ivan Barbashev, 47 seconds later, deflected a point shot from Shea Theodore for a 3-1 lead.

Coupled with Brossoit making at least three key saves in the period, the Golden Knights went into the third in an eerily similar situation from Game 3: a solid second period that took the crowd out of it and a multigoal lead.

"We all knew it was going to be a way tougher game today," Barbashev said. "We knew they were going to give their best."

But the Jets played their part to make it similar to Game 3. Pierre-Luc Dubois scored 2:57 into the third, on the power play, thanks to a fortuitous bounce where the puck popped high above the net and floated over Brossoit's shoulder.

That was the only blunder — if you could call it that — on Brossoit's ledger.

Brossoit earned his way to the starting job for Vegas in the playoffs. Not that he'll ever admit if he was nervous. His businesslike mentality will never give that away.

But the Golden Knights were able to fend off a late Winnipeg rally because of their "backup" goalie.

On the organizational pecking order, Brossoit might be the No. 2. Right now, he's anything but that. And he's one more win from sending his former team home for the summer.

"He's a fantastic goalie," Theodore said. "He's on his game right now." ■

Alex Pietrangelo (7) and Pierre-Luc Dubois (80) reach for a bouncing puck in front of goaltender Laurent Brossoit during the third period of Game 4. (AP Images)

PURE CHEMISTRY

Stone and Stephenson Strike Early, Push Golden Knights to Second Round

By Danny Webster

The chemistry between Mark Stone and Chandler Stephenson may never be understood.

The Golden Knights' two All-Star forwards can't comprehend it. Something just works when they skate together, as if they're of the same brain and know where they're going to be at all times.

Understandably so, it was going to take time for Stone to get back to his old self. Stephenson helped accelerate that process.

Stephenson scored twice — his first multigoal playoff game — and Stone had a goal and two assists to push the Golden Knights into the second round of the Stanley Cup Playoffs with a 4-1 win over the Winnipeg Jets.

"Sometimes you just find chemistry with a guy," Stone said.

It's one thing to find that chemistry and keep it going. It's another entirely to have that chemistry over the course of three years since Stephenson arrived from Washington in December 2019 and make it work.

Then, you factor in Stone undergoing his second back surgery in less than a year, being away for three months, but coming back and seemingly not missing a beat.

That's what Games 2-5 of this series showed, as Vegas became the first team in the field of 16 to advance to the second round.

Stephenson has a Stanley Cup-winning pedigree, but not at this level. He was a fourth liner in 2018 with the Capitals and had seven points through 24 games that year.

In these five games against the Jets, he had eight points (four goals, four assists). He also joined former line mate Max Pacioretty as the only two Golden Knights to register four consecutive multipoint games.

"Confidence just built and built," Stephenson said about his arrival, going from 33 points in five years in Washington to nearly 200 with Vegas in three-plus seasons. "When you play with Stoney and Patch, it helps."

Stone, too, has found that confidence in his game with an eight-point series. He registered his second three-point game of the series in the deciding contest.

The line of Stone, Stephenson and left winger Brett Howden carried the offense in three of the Golden Knights' victories in their four-game run after losing Game 1, 5-1.

Chandler Stephenson celebrates with his teammates after scoring during the first period of Game 5. (Wade Vandervort / Las Vegas Sun)

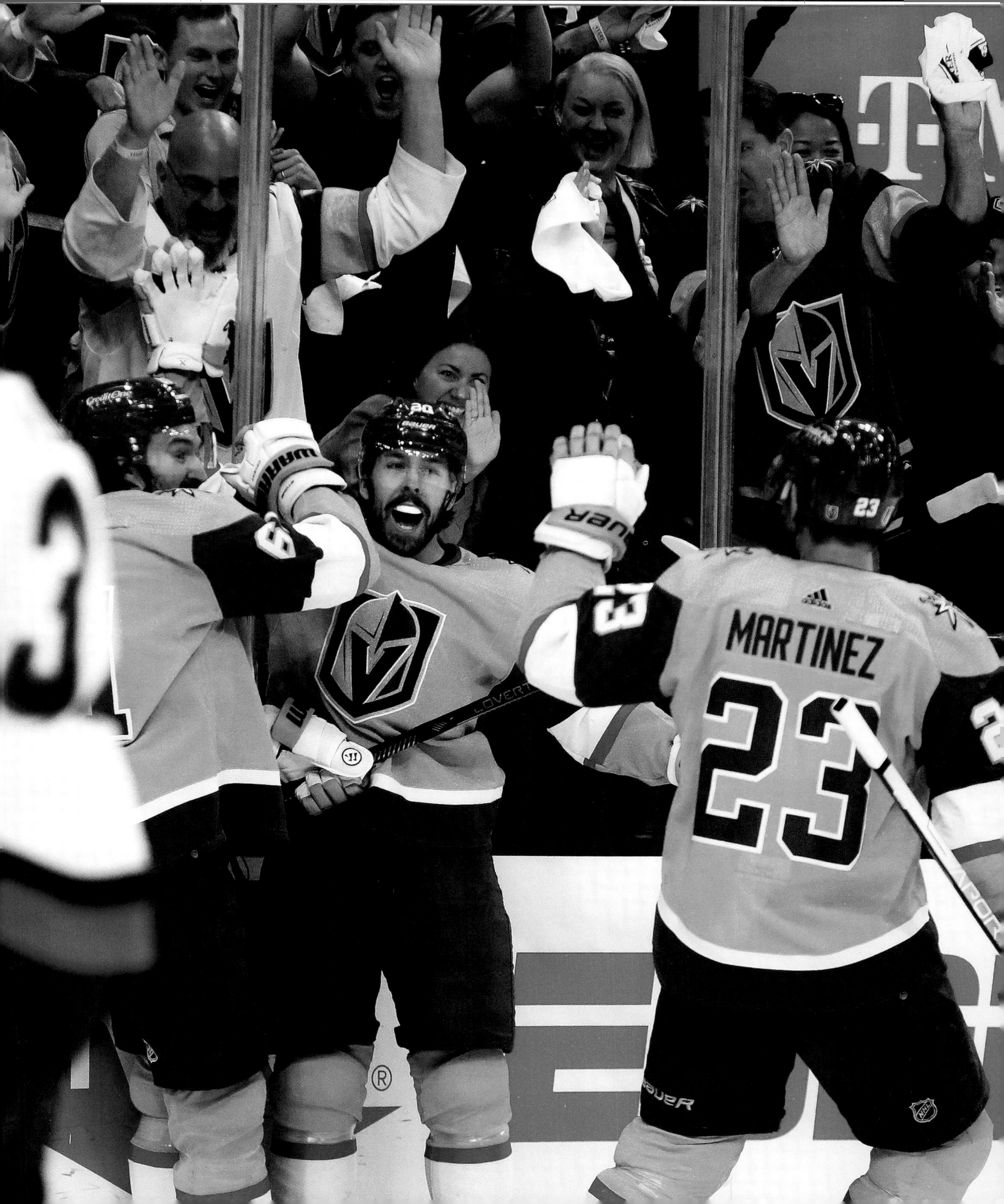
MARTINEZ
23

William Karlsson added his fourth goal of the series in the win, and Laurent Brossoit made 30 saves to defeat his former team and goalie partner Connor Hellebuyck. Brossoit played three seasons in Winnipeg before signing with Vegas in 2021.

Vegas outscored Winnipeg 18-9 in Games 2-5.

"We had a game plan we wanted to stick with until it didn't work, which it never didn't work," Stone said. "I think we accomplished what we wanted to accomplish."

With all the good that came with Vegas winning its eighth playoff series in six years, the good news offset some of the bad that arrived prior to puck drop.

The Golden Knights were down two of their top four defensemen. Brayden McNabb (upper body) is day-to-day, and Shea Theodore was a late scratch due to an illness. AHL Henderson captain Brayden Pachal and 30-year-old Ben Hutton played their first Stanley Cup Playoff games.

But for all the scratches, Vegas was healthiest at the forward position for the first time since the beginning of the season.

William Carrier returned to the lineup for the first time since March 3 with a lower-body injury. It's the first time since the beginning of the season where the Golden Knights had all forwards healthy and accounted for. Carrier replaced Phil Kessel, who was not in the lineup in an NHL game for the first time since Nov. 3, 2009.

Carrier played 9:52, but had two shots on goal and a team-high six hits.

Even with those changes, it still might have been the Golden Knights' best performance all series. This time, it took 50 seconds to set the tone.

After an extended stint in the offensive zone, Stephenson scored his third goal of the series on a tap-in from Stone less than a minute into the game for a 1-0 lead.

Stephenson's goal was the third fastest to open a playoff game in team history (Stone: 0:19 (R1, G3 - 2019), Jonathan Marchessault: 0:35 (R3, G3 - 2018).

Winnipeg looked like a team that was already defeated rather than trying to fight for its playoff life. The Golden Knights were first to every loose puck, first to win every battle. The relentless pressure carried, even with the Golden Knights down two significant pieces on their blue line.

The snowball kept rolling in the second period.

Stone caught an airborne puck in the offensive zone, settled it down, and beat Hellebuyck glove side 42 seconds into the middle frame for a 2-0 lead.

Karlsson scored his fourth of the series at 4:41 off a backhand pass from Michael Amadio to make it 3-0, and Stephenson scored his second — a power-play goal at 8:37 — to make it 4-0.

"I don't think we gave up much," coach Bruce Cassidy said. "I thought it was our closest to complete, but we still have things to work on."

Cassidy was asked Wednesday about taking a team's soul when it's on the ropes. The Golden Knights' coach preferred to be asked that after Game 5.

While the answer was vague at the time, what happened in the first 40 minutes might be the closest thing to it.

One thing's for sure: The Golden Knights are going into Round 2 with a healthy Stone and an effective Stephenson playing on the third line. Not many teams can match that.

"I think a lot of people were questioning us after Game 1, and maybe after the first period in Game 2," Stone said. "But we took over." ∎

Michael Amadio vies for the puck with Winnipeg Jets defenseman Nate Schmidt. (Wade Vandervort / Las Vegas Sun)

Wade Vandervort / Las Vegas Sun

✦ WESTERN CONFERENCE SEMIFINAL GAME 1 ✦
May 3, 2023 • Las Vegas, Nevada
Golden Knights 6, Oilers 4

GAME CHANGER

With Mark Stone in Top Form, Golden Knights Dull Oilers' Star Power

By Case Keefer

Mark Stone crouched down and shimmied his shoulders in his final move on the ice following the Vegas Golden Knights' 6-4 Game 1 victory over the Edmonton Oilers.

It was a far more graceful and joyous rink exit than he managed the previous morning at City National Arena when the 30-year-old labored out of practice in a manner that had fans fearing he tweaked a chronic back injury. Stone quelled those concerns a day later by leading the upset of the Oilers with yet another stat-stuffing performance in his sixth game back from surgery to address the aforementioned back issue in January.

He led the Golden Knights' forwards in ice time (19:46), put up two points (one goal and one assist) and forced two takeaways.

"It's no surprise, obviously," Vegas defenseman Zach Whitecloud said. "Mark Stone, this time of year, you've got guys that have a switch and can just flip it and it's playoff time. To be able to get (Stone) back in our lineup and the way he leads, the way he plays the game of hockey, leads us as a team, his energy, talking, the way he handles pucks, the way he defends..."

Whitecloud's endorsement of Stone went on a bit longer, but you get the point: It was effusive. And it felt somewhat out of place as most of the Golden Knights who spoke postgame saved more superlatives for their opponents than their teammates.

"Talented" and "dangerous" were the buzz words regarding the Oilers, and must have been muttered 100 times between the Golden Knights' locker room and their news conference. Vegas' players seemed to be nothing but sincere, but part of you has to be hoping that they're actually seething inside while sharing the compliments. That they're really being as theatrical as Stone in his much-discussed celebrations to avoid rolling their eyes or laughing off all the talk about Edmonton's "top-end" — another phrase at least one Golden Knight used — personnel.

The recent gushing over the Oilers is even more over the top by analysts, and implicit in the praise is the insinuation that the Golden Knights aren't on the same level.

That's wrong.

It was Vegas that won the Pacific Division after all, albeit by the slimmest of margins (two points)

Having undergone back surgery earlier in the season, Mark Stone returned to top form during the playoffs, scoring in the first period Game 1 against the Edmonton Oilers. (Steve Marcus / Las Vegas Sun)

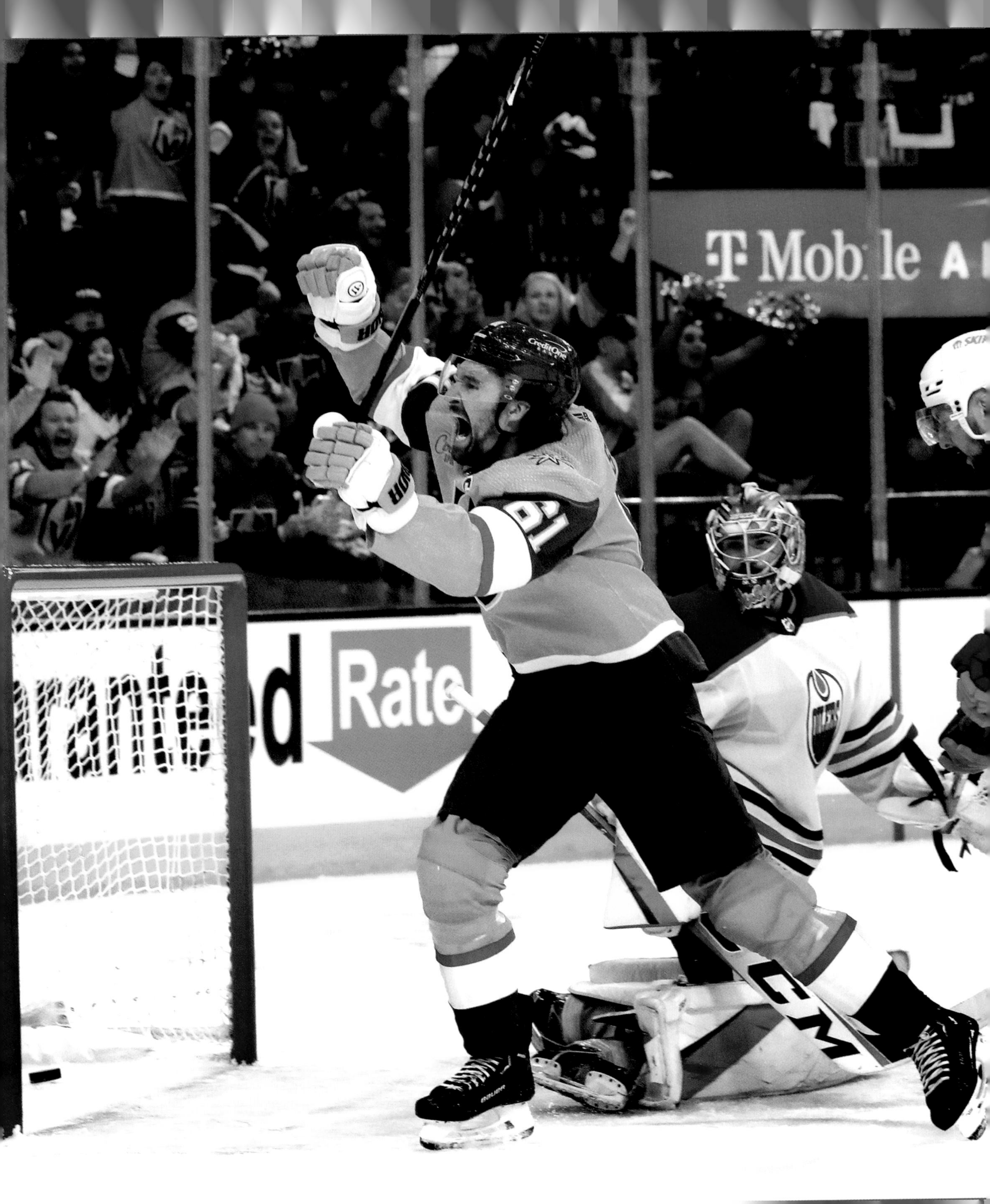
T Mobile
Rate

that more advanced numbers indicated was probably undeserved. But the billing of this series for the right to go to the Western Conference Final would lead anyone to believe that the Golden Knights are like the Mighty Ducks — either the motley original 1992 Disney fictional version or the very real 2022-2023 Anaheim team that finished with the league's worst record — next to the all-world Oilers.

They're neither that ragtag nor even anything like the franchise's original "misfit" team that famously reached the Stanley Cup Final five years ago. The Golden Knights may not have two of the world's very best players like the Oilers' Leon Draisaitl, who scored all four of the team's goals in Game 1, and Connor McDavid, but they're also not lacking for star power.

"There are special players that do special things," Vegas coach Bruce Cassidy said when asked about Draisaitl. "We have some of those (too)."

None are more special than Stone, who's spent the early portion of the playoffs reminding everyone of that fact. The winger is leading the team with 10 postseason points despite looking "rusty," in Cassidy's words, to start the first-round series against Winnipeg in his first action in nearly five months.

No, Stone may not be as flashy as McDavid, Draisaitl or even Vegas teammate Jack Eichel, who like Stone had a goal and assist to start the Edmonton series. Eichel is getting most of the media attention on the Vegas side because of the way he's forever linked with McDavid as the top two picks of the 2015 NHL Draft.

But Stone remains Vegas' best player. And there's no one playing on either side of the series who's as much of a game-changer both offensively and defensively.

It's amazing that Stone has so effortlessly regained his form after all the time away, and that he maintained it despite the Oilers' best efforts in Game 1. News of Stone's potential re-aggravated injury had clearly and unsurprisingly reached Edmonton as the visitors targeted him with a series of early big hits.

The Golden Knights began protesting some borderline crosschecking on Stone, and the constant barrage diminished, if only slightly.

"It hurts to win and Stoney is a big example of that," Whitecloud said. "He's taken a lot and he doesn't retaliate. He does that sort of thing, and that feeds through our lineup."

Stone's impact may go beyond any quantifiable number, and hopefully can be on display throughout the rest of the Golden Knights' postseason run. He hasn't spoken to the media since the apparent practice scare, but Cassidy has insisted he's fine and demonstrated as much by giving the captain his normal allotment of ice time to start the series with Edmonton.

As long as Stone is playing, the Golden Knights are nowhere close to overmatched. It's going to be a tight series regardless, one Draisaitl and McDavid may well steal despite the Stone-led Game 1 win.

But the Golden Knights are in a fairer fight than some of the descriptions of both teams would lead you to believe. This isn't a stars versus scrubs series.

"We're aware of their top guys and the damage they can do, but we like our team," Cassidy said. "We feel that if our team plays well, then we'll have success." ∎

Chandler Stephenson scored during the third period of the Golden Knights' 6-4 win. (Steve Marcus / Las Vegas Sun)

LACK OF COHESION

Cassidy Says Golden Knights Were 'Out-Teammated' in Disappointing Game 2

By Danny Webster

There's 2:18 remaining in the second period, and a melee ensues.

It starts at center ice with Golden Knights forward Brett Howden and Edmonton Oilers defenseman Brett Kulak dropping the gloves. More fisticuffs take place in the top left corner of the rink where Keegan Kolesar is getting drilled in the mid-section by Edmonton's Evander Kane.

Referee Kelly Sutherland stands by and watches, notebook in hand, as Kane continues after the whistle.

That sequence isn't why the Golden Knights lost 5-1 in Game 2 of their second-round series to the Oilers, tying the series at a game apiece. The technicalities of Connor McDavid and Leon Draisaitl taking over on the power play more than did the damage there.

But the barrage of goals for Edmonton wasn't the worst part of the night for Bruce Cassidy.

"You're going to have nights you're going to get out-executed, especially against this team," said the Golden Knights' coach. "They were more competitive, but we got sort of out-teammated for lack of a better term. That's disappointing. It should never happen to the Vegas Golden Knights."

The Golden Knights knew the pushback from the Oilers was coming. This was more than a push. More than a shove.

After falling behind early thanks to a four-goal onslaught in the first period, they got punched in the mouth, and then some.

The frustration was evident, ranging from Cassidy to the locker room, that the Golden Knights didn't do enough to stand up for Kolesar, someone the Golden Knights view as the one who stands up for his teammates on nearly every occasion that calls for it.

It was still frustrating for Mark Stone to see Sutherland standing within feet of Kolesar getting leveled without doing anything.

"The ref's standing right there. We only got four guys, they got five, and the refs are just standing there letting him get hit," Stone said. "You never want to see a teammate getting suckered down like that, especially for a guy who's stuck up for his teammates like he has all year. We would've liked to see the refs do a little more of their job to help Keegan."

More importantly from an on-ice perspective, the Oilers tied the best-of-7 series 1-1 with the series shifting to Alberta for Game 3.

The Golden Knights knew they weren't going to sweep the Oilers. As long as McDavid and Draisaitl keep skating, the Oilers are never out of anything.

Edmonton's superstars set the tone in Game 2. McDavid and Draisaitl each scored twice time with the two providing three of the Oilers' four goals in the first period.

The Oilers' first two goals came by way of the power play — one by Draisaitl, the other by Evan Bouchard — and McDavid contributed with a shorthanded goal in the first 11:11 of the game.

Cassidy said the responsibility falls on the coaching staff for not having the Golden Knights ready to start.

"They were a lot better than us. They were ready to play. We weren't, for whatever reason," Cassidy said.

Draisaitl, who had four goals in Game 1, opened the scoring 2:21 into the game on a power-play goal. Much like in Game 1, the Golden Knights committed a penalty less than two minutes into the game. This time, Brayden McNabb's cross-checking infraction resulted in Draisaitl's goal.

Bouchard scored Edmonton's second power-play goal at 7:01 for a 2-0 lead after a high-sticking penalty called on Zach Whitecloud.

Draisaitl added his second — his 13th of the playoffs and sixth of the series — at 16:17 to extend Edmonton's lead to 4-0.

The Oilers, who had a record-setting power play during the regular season at 32.4%, are 5 for 9 in the series on the man advantage after a 3 for 6 outing on Saturday. McDavid, who led to the league with 64 goals in the regular season, scored 11:43 into the second to make 5-0.

Vegas' best chance in this series, as it showed in Game 1, is keeping the game at 5-on-5. It's easier said than done against Edmonton's power play, but Cassidy reaffirms the need to be better when shorthanded.

"They were better than us in special teams. Whatever the penalties were, it doesn't matter. They scored on them," Cassidy said. "We've got to find a way

to A) limit those, and B) doing a better job at killing them. Which is not an easy task. We know that."

The Golden Knights got on the board 1:36 into the third on Ivan Barbashev's third goal of the series, but that was all they could generate.

Laurent Brossoit made 27 saves on 32 shots before being pulled for Adin Hill in the third. While five goals against will look bad on paper, falling behind in that fashion was far from Brossoit's fault.

The Golden Knights entered the postseason as the least-penalized team in the league (273 penalties), but that hasn't mattered at all to the Oilers. Edmonton has found a way to capitalize, even in moments where the structure within Vegas' penalty-killing unit was good.

"We're doing a lot of good things on the kill, but they're dynamic," Stone said.

Now, the Golden Knights go on the road. In hindsight, that's a good thing. Vegas was one of the best road teams in the regular season (26-7-8) and swept Games 3 and 4 in Winnipeg in the first round. There's reason to feel confident there.

Obvious as it may seem, the Jets aren't the Oilers. They've converted on their chances. They currently have the hottest goal scorer on the planet. All signs point to the pendulum swinging back to the Oilers favor heading home after a split.

Cassidy is confident that the execution and the compete level will come back for the Golden Knights, much like it did in the Winnipeg series, but the team-togetherness needs to return above anything else.

"You're not going to win if you're not going to play as a team," Cassidy said. "The competitive spirit that's in our group was not here today. It'll come back." ∎

May 8, 2023 • Edmonton, Alberta
Golden Knights 5, Oilers 1

ROAD WARRIORS

Marchessault Snaps Slump, Golden Knights Overcome Loss of Brossoit in Game 3

By Danny Webster

The question was posed to Bruce Cassidy after Game 2: Could it be beneficial for the Golden Knights to get their depth scoring, knowing Jonathan Marchessault hadn't found the back of the net yet in the playoffs?

Vegas' leading scorer didn't score in that loss at home. He made up for it in Game 3.

Marchessault scored twice, his first goals this postseason, and the Golden Knights responded with a 5-1 win over the Edmonton Oilers at Rogers Place to take a 2-1 lead in this second-round series.

"It was nice to just help the team win a game," Marchessault said. "When the goals don't come and you get chances, it's a matter of time where it's going to come."

Jack Eichel had a goal and two assists, and Vegas overcame losing goalie Laurent Brossoit in the first period to a noncontact lower-body injury.

Adin Hill stopped all 25 shots he faced in relief of Brossoit in his first extended action since March 7.

"Just try to be patient and stay on my feet as long as I can," said Hill, who himself suffered a lower-body injury that cost him the final month of the regular season. "Just tracking the puck and being patient, and I feel like when I do that, I'm at the top of my game.

"Before I got hurt there, I was doing a really good job of that and I feel like I kind of picked up where I left off."

Chandler Stephenson scored his team-leading sixth goal of the playoffs, and Zach Whitecloud added his first playoff goal in 20 games in a much-needed response for the Golden Knights.

Vegas, after winning 6-4 in Game 1, fell behind early thanks to a four-goal first period by the Oilers in Game 2 and lost in a final tally of 5-1.

This win pushed the Golden Knights to 3-0 on the road in the postseason.

"All year, our group has had a next-man-in mentality. If we score a goal or get scored on, the next shift is important," Marchessault said. "It's one of those teams where if you have a one-goal lead or a two-goal lead, they're never down."

Referee Kyle Rehman tries to get a view of the action as the Vegas Golden Knights and Edmonton Oilers battle at the Knights' net. (AP Images)

Edmonton went 3 for 6 on the power play in Game 2 after going 2 for 3 in Game 1. The Oilers had a record-setting 32.4% power play during the regular season.

Not only did the Oilers go 0 for 3 on the power play on Monday, but neither of the first two attempts came with a full two minutes.

Edmonton's final power play with five minutes remaining was the only instance where the Oilers got a full two minutes, which the Golden Knights successfully killed off.

"Everyone knows how great their power play is," Eichel said. "We did a good job of that, checking with our legs. You just want to continue to do that over the next few games."

The Golden Knights kept the game to 5-on-5, and it paid off, thanks to Marchessault.

Vegas' leading goal scorer during the regular season (28) scored 1:59 after Warren Foegele opened the scoring for Edmonton (2:45) to tie it 1-1. Eichel found Marchessault for his second goal at 19:09 of the first for a 2-1 Vegas lead that the road team wouldn't relinquish.

Whitecloud increased the lead to two at 7:25 of the second when his shot hit the top right corner of the net, over Edmonton's Stuart Skinner's shoulder. It was Whitecloud's first playoff goal in almost nearly two years to the day (Game 7 vs. Minnesota, May 28, 2021).

Eichel made it 4-1 less than five minutes later after evading defenseman Evan Bouchard in the neutral zone and beat Skinner on a 2-on-1. That goal ended Skinner's night with the Calder Trophy finalist giving up four goals on 23 shots.

Stephenson scored at 17:13 of the second, deflecting a shot past Jack Campbell for the 5-1 lead.

Keeping it 5-on-5 also limited Edmonton stars Connor McDavid and Leon Draisaitl in their production.

The two combined for six shots on goal and were a minus-4 at 5-on-5.

Draisaitl leads all players in the postseason with 13 goals, including six in the first two games of the series.

Going into Monday, the Golden Knights had eight different goal scorers through seven playoff games. All of them were forwards, and none of them were Marchessault, or even from a defenseman.

Whitecloud's goal was the first from a defenseman this postseason.

"One night it's going to be one guy, another night it's going to be another guy," Marchessault said. "It's how you build a winning team, and that's the mentality we have this year."

But Cassidy said Marchessault — and to that extent, Reilly Smith (also without a goal this postseason) — was going to find his opportunities to score. He got his best chance in a rebounding effort.

Game 4 is coming. Goalie? Unknown. Outcome? Unknown. But the Golden Knights stole back home-ice advantage in their own emphatic way. ∎

Jonathan Marchessault scored twice during the 5-1 win, his first goals of the 2023 playoffs. (AP Images)

✦ WESTERN CONFERENCE SEMIFINAL GAME 4 ✦
May 10, 2023 • Edmonton, Alberta
Oilers 4, Golden Knights 1

SLASH AND BURN

Tempers Flare Late in Golden Knights' Game 4 Loss to Oilers

By Danny Webster

If it usually takes one, maybe two moments in a playoff game to spark a rivalry, the final 10 minutes of Game 4 between the Golden Knights and Edmonton Oilers had about five of them.

Players are swinging their hockey sticks like baseball bats. Cross-checks to the face as blatant as the eye can see. Fights with less than a minute to go. All the hilarity you could expect in a second-round series that is now down to a best-of-3.

Yet, as the Golden Knights lost 4-1 in Game 4 at Rogers Place, tying their series with Edmonton at 2-2, the talk should be focused on how Vegas got severely outplayed for the first time in this back-and-forth series. More on that later.

Right now, the aftermath goes to what could be to come in the all-important Game 5 back at T-Mobile Arena.

Golden Knights defenseman Alex Pietrangelo was assessed a five-minute major and game misconduct with 1:27 remaining in the game for slashing — in this case, swinging his stick like a baseball bat — at Edmonton star Leon Draisaitl.

Moments later, Oilers defenseman Darnell Nurse instigated a fight with Vegas' Nicolas Hague, and both were removed from the game.

Nurse's situation, by rule, could lead to a one-game suspension according to Rule 46.21 in the NHL's rulebook.

While there's no rule that says Pietrangelo could serve a suspension for slashing, the likelihood of him getting a call from the NHL's Department of Player Safety today is high.

Whether or not suspensions could be coming, the Golden Knights missed a chance to seize control of the series.

This was the Golden Knights' chance to put the pressure on the Oilers after a dominant Game 3 victory. How Vegas played that game — keeping it 5-on-5, keeping Edmonton's stars away from the middle of the ice — was a perfect response after losing Game 2, 5-1.

But as has been the case this entire series between the Pacific Division's top two teams, neither team wants to grab momentum.

After Vegas' thrilling 6-4 win in Game 1, the Oilers pushed back for the resounding 5-1 win in Game 2. The Golden Knights answered with a pushback of their own in Game 3, winning by the same margin as in Game 2 and playing their most complete game of the series.

"You chalk it up to two really good hockey teams that have just outplayed one or the other," defenseman Alec Martinez said.

Game 4 was the Oilers' most complete effort by far.

Edmonton, which had been outplayed at 5-on-5 all

series, scored three times at even strength and needed only one power-play goal. But much like Game 2, the Golden Knights fell behind early and couldn't recover.

Nick Bjugstad (6:46) and Evan Bouchard (7:38) scored 52 seconds apart in the first period to give the Oilers a 2-0 lead. Mattias Ekholm (13:30) made it 3-0 Edmonton.

It wasn't as lethal as Game 2, where the Oilers scored two power-play goals and a shorthanded goal by Connor McDavid as part of a four-goal first period.

This was more effective, though. The Oilers got goals from their top two defensemen and a middle-six forward, with McDavid and Draisaitl recording one assist each.

"I don't think it was our greatest night on the forecheck," captain Mark Stone said. "We've got to be ready for Friday night."

Meanwhile, the Golden Knights' game that was successful in Game 3 couldn't materialize. The Oilers were the more physical team, out-hitting Vegas 46-36. The Golden Knights were outshot 24-13 at 5-on-5 and out-attempted 37-26.

The Golden Knights also had just one high-danger chance at even strength through two periods.

But that's not to say they didn't have their opportunities.

The Golden Knights had three of their four power-play opportunities in the second period; two of them came consecutively from 7:57 to 10:02 of the frame, but they failed to capitalize. The Oilers did, however, when Ryan Nugent-Hopkins scored his first goal of the postseason at 14:45 to make it 4-0.

"If we move the puck quicker, we don't put ourselves in those spots," coach Bruce Cassidy said. "We're one of the final eight teams in the playoffs. If you're not ready to play and you don't expect that, you're going to be in trouble."

It wound up being a night to forget for Adin Hill in his first career playoff start. He made 29 saves, but the shots he saw were far more dangerous than the 24 he stopped in relief of Laurent Brossoit in Game 3.

At the other end, Edmonton rookie Stuart Skinner rebounded after being pulled in Game 3 with a 25-save effort. It would've been a perfect night for Skinner had Nicolas Roy's goal at 5:58 of the third ended the shutout bid.

The Golden Knights entered the playoffs as the least-penalized team in the league at 273 penalties (583 penalty minutes). Games 2 and 4 saw a combined 134 penalty minutes for the Golden Knights; 56 of their 64 in Game 4 came in the third period when hilarity ensued.

On top of Pietrangelo getting tossed from the game, Chandler Stephenson was given a 10-minute misconduct at 12:55 for holding Kailer Yamamoto's stick from the bench.

Jonathan Marchessault was given a game misconduct for retaliation against Oilers forward Evander Kane for cross-checking Pietrangelo earlier in the period. Brett Howden was given a misconduct late for goalie interference.

If the bad blood wasn't evident before, it is now.

This seesaw series now returns to Las Vegas. The pendulum favors no one. Both teams have a win at home and on the road. The Oilers have a 14-13 scoring edge in a series that has seen three games decided by three goals or more.

Much like the rest of the second round, this series has made no sense. Game 5 is the ultimate swing game. And somehow, this seems far from over.

"It's a bit of what happens in the playoffs," Cassidy said. "Temperature goes up as the series goes along. It'll probably go up some more in Game 5." ■

May 12, 2023 • Las Vegas, Nevada
Golden Knights 4, Oilers 3

NOT THIS TIME

Golden Knights Fend Off Major Penalty to Take Control of Series

By Case Keefer

The same memory from four years ago flooded nearly everyone's minds at T-Mobile Arena when Golden Knights forward Keegan Kolesar took a five-minute major penalty for boarding the Edmonton Oilers' Mattias Ekholm.

A similar late-game call infamously and controversially ended Vegas' Stanley Cup Playoff run in 2019 by helping to wipe out a two-goal lead against the San Jose Sharks. Was history going to painfully repeat?

The situation was surely "stressful," in forward Jonathan Marchessault's words, for the 18,590 fans in attendance, but the players weren't immune to feeling the similarities either, at least not the handful of players who were on the 2019 team. Forward Reilly Smith went out of his way not to explicitly address to the previous loss after the game but alluded to it multiple times.

"You're aware of situations (because) you only get so many opportunities in the playoffs," Smith said in the dressing room. "So, to have things slip away like that is pretty tough. We did a better job this time."

A gutsy five-minute penalty kill that stretched for 20 seconds at the end of the second period into the start of the third period ultimately led Vegas to a 4-3 victory over Edmonton in Game 5 of the Western Conference semifinal series. The Golden Knights gave up one goal to Connor McDavid during the stretch, but otherwise went unscathed to take a 3-2 series lead into Game 6 at Edmonton.

Turning away the Oilers' other six shots was no small feat considering the visitors have the best man-advantage in the history of the NHL statistically. Edmonton's power play had already chipped in eight goals throughout the series including a pair in the first period of Game 5.

And Vegas goalie Adin Hill, with all due respect, wouldn't figure to be as sure of a stopper as future Hall of Famer Marc-Andre Fleury four years ago against the Sharks. Hill made his second playoff start, after returning from a lower-body injury and taking over for Laurent Brossoit after the goalie went down in a Game 3 loss. It went much more smoothly this outing after his first start in the 4-1 beatdown in Edmonton in Game 4.

But he said he felt he "picked up where he left off" with 32 saves on the night. The score only went from 4-2 to 4-3 with him locked in during the major penalty behind an attacking defense — much different than when San Jose went from down 3-1 to up 4-3 in Game 7 of the 2019 first-round series.

"That could have been a turning point in the game

Reilly Smith skates against Edmonton Oilers center Ryan Nugent-Hopkins during the third period. Smith scored on a pass from William Karlsson in the hard-fought 4-3 win. (Steve Marcus / Las Vegas Sun)

big-time, and we got through it," Vegas coach Bruce Cassidy said in his postgame news conference. "Even though we lost the special-teams battle, three to two, I think in reality, in our minds, we won it. That's how we look at it. On five-on-five, our game is solid."

The Golden Knights have outplayed the Oilers at even strength for the majority of the five games so far, but they also held their own on special teams despite the inauspicious start. Vegas had three first-period power play opportunities but failed to capitalize on any of them to drop its rate to 2-for-18 on the series at the time. Edmonton's two early power-play goals, on the other hand, came relatively easily with McDavid and Zach Hyman scoring right in front of the net.

Everything changed in the second period when the Oilers picked up back-to-back whistles — a holding call on Philip Broberg followed by a high-sticking on Mattias Ekholm — to give the Golden Knights a 5-on-3 advantage.

That was enough to break them out of their power-play funk, as Mark Stone forced a goal in from the paint in front of Stuart Skinner to tie the game at 2-2.

Then, 29 seconds later, Reilly Smith converted on a pinpoint pass from William Karlsson inches from the net to give the Golden Knights their first lead of the night.

The onslaught didn't end there. Nicolas Hague added another score, firing a puck past Skinner's left side from the blue line to put the Golden Knights up 4-2.

The three goals came in a total of 1:29 of game time, the fastest a trio of scores have come in franchise playoff history.

"I thought we did some good things tonight, but in the end, that segment in the second period hobbled us and we weren't able to get it done," Oilers coach Jay Woodcroft said.

The home crowd erupted louder than it has all postseason, but celebrations were cut short five minutes later when Kolesar viciously forced Ekholm into the boards. Dirty plays and scuffles were far fewer in Game 5 than in Game 4, which included Vegas defenseman Alex Pietrangelo slashing Edmonton superstar Leon Draisaitl late to draw a one-game suspension served Friday, but Kolesar's penalty definitely fell in the former category. And it's a wonder it didn't cause a bout of the latter.

Ekholm was helped off the ice but later returned in the third period.

The Golden Knights went all-out to prevent Kolesar's mistake from sinking them, flinging their bodies at shots and following Cassidy's words at the second intermission to be aggressive in going after the Oilers.

"We've been in that situation before where they can really hurt you, so we're obviously pretty cognizant that you can't let those momentum shifts slide," Smith said. "We did a good job. We kept them to the outside, tired them out and we took a lot of momentum out of it."

Vegas kept limiting Edmonton's chances for the rest of the period with their forecheck and puck possession. The Oilers weren't able to pull goalie Jack Campbell, who came in for Skinner after Hague's goal, for an extra skater until two minutes remained because of how long the Golden Knights controlled the puck in their zone.

The Golden Knights blocked a couple more shots, and Hill turned a few away to secure the victory. For one night at least, "five-minute major" can't count as a cursed phrase for the Golden Knights.

On the contrary, managing such a penalty lifted Vegas to being one victory away from the fourth Western Conference Final berth in the franchise's six-year history."

"We knew we could use that five-minute penalty as a momentum swing for us if we killed it properly, and I think one goal out of five minutes for us was a win," Marchessault said. "We battled through adversity and just kept going." ∎

Defenseman Nicolas Hague celebrates with Jack Eichel after scoring the third of three Golden Knights goals during the second period. (Steve Marcus / Las Vegas Sun)

HALFWAY THERE

Marchessault's Hat Trick Sends Golden Knights to Western Conference Final

By Danny Webster

Jonathan Marchessault has arguably been the Golden Knights' most impactful playoff performer since the team's inaugural season. It took him some time to heat up this postseason, but he delivered once again in Game 6 to send Vegas back to the NHL's final four.

Marchessault recorded a natural hat trick in the second period — his second career playoff hat trick. With it, the Golden Knights are moving on to the Western Conference Final for the fourth time in their six-year history, notching a 5-2 win over the Edmonton Oilers to cap their second-round series at Rogers Place.

"This year, I got to say, it's been really special," Marchessault said on the ESPN postgame broadcast. "We definitely have a good thing going on."

Given how the Golden Knights breezed through their five-game series against Winnipeg in the first round, it's easy to understand how those who didn't get on the score sheet — Marchessault among them — were overlooked.

Marchessault, who had 28 goals to lead Vegas during the regular season, had a quiet two assists in those five games. Going seven playoff games without a goal was uncharacteristic for him.

He broke through in Game 3 against Edmonton with two goals in a 5-1 win. After no points in Game 4, he had three assists in the 4-3 Game 5 win.

Now was his time to be the hero.

"He had a huge series. He had a great night tonight," center Jack Eichel said of Marchessault. "Well deserved."

The script on Sunday night was eerily similar to the first five games. The Golden Knights found themselves trailing against the highest-scoring team in the NHL after the first period.

But Game 6 provided a plot twist. Reilly Smith scored 24 seconds into the game, the first time the Golden Knights scored first in a game all series, for a 1-0 lead. That advantage lasted 31 seconds before Connor McDavid tied it on the first shot goalie Adin Hill saw.

The second shot Hill saw came at 2:43 on a one-timer from Warren Foegele to give the Oilers a 2-1 lead.

Vegas ended the first period trailing by one. Given a shaky defensive performance, the score could have been much worse. Edmonton outshot Vegas 15-7.

What turned the game in the Golden Knights' favor was the first five minutes of the second period. Though Vegas was heavily outshot, they controlled possession with extended shifts in the offensive zone.

After a slow start to the 2023 playoffs, Jonathan Marchessault scored a natural hat trick in the second period of Game 6 against the Oilers. (AP Images)

"In the end, you need timely goals and timely saves. We got those tonight."
—Coach Bruce Cassidy

The line of William Karlsson, Nicolas Roy and Smith had a 47-second shift, with three shots on goal starting from the 16:58 mark. On the next shift, Jack Eichel's line with Ivan Barbashev and Marchessault kept possession for 37 seconds, resulting in Marchessault's first goal at 4:26 to tie the score 2-2.

The Eichel-Barbashev-Marchessault trio was on the ice for 1:09 on their next shift three minutes later. That ended with Marchessault's second goal at 7:44 off a rebound from Alec Martinez's point shot for a 3-2 Vegas lead.

Marchessault capped off the hat trick with a 4-on-4 goal at 18:36 for the 4-2 lead. His 26 playoff points as a member of the Golden Knights are the most in team history, passing Mark Stone (23).

"Everyone out here is just trying to play the right way," Marchessault said. "Sometimes you get rewarded. One night it's one guy, another night it's another guy."

Vegas wouldn't have gotten the chance to carry a two-goal lead had it not been for Hill's performance. After allowing two goals, Hill stopped the next 38 shots he faced to preserve his third win since Game 3.

In five appearances this series, Hill has gone 3-1 with a 2.19 goals-against average and .934 save percentage on 136 shots faced.

"He was incredible," defenseman Nic Hague said of Hill. "We knew we needed a couple of big saves. They weren't going to go away without a big push. When we did break down, Hilly came through with a handful."

The Golden Knights have been confident that they can play their same game no matter who is in goal. This time, Hill needed to bail out his teammates. Edmonton had a 15-7 edge in high-danger chances and 3.81 expected goals at 5-on-5.

"In the end, you need timely goals and timely saves," coach Bruce Cassidy said. "We got those tonight."

William Karlsson's empty-net goal with 39 seconds remaining capped a night where all members of the Misfit Line scored. Even though they're on separate lines, Marchessault, Karlsson and Smith each had their handprints on this series.

Neither member of Edmonton's superstar tandem, Leon Draisaitl and McDavid, scored a goal when defended by Karlsson. Smith, playing on that same line, also aided defensively but scored his first two goals of the postseason — the go-ahead goal in Game 5, and then on Sunday.

The trio — three of the six left who played in the Stanley Cup Final in the inaugural season — will get another chance to get back.

"We're going to enjoy it tonight," Marchessault said, "but we're just halfway done." ∎

Alex Pietrangelo and Edmonton Oilers' Zach Hyman battle for the puck during the decisive second-round game. (AP Images)

ONE MOVE AHEAD

It's Time to Start Praising the Golden Knights' Maligned Front Office

By Case Keefer • May 25, 2023

Bruce Cassidy recused himself from conversations involving Adin Hill when the Golden Knights began zoning in on the 27-year-old goaltender as a trade target before the season. Vegas' first-year coach says he "knew very little about" the then-San Jose Sharks' backup, whom Cassidy never encountered during his stint coaching the Boston Bruins, so he felt it would be better if the front office handled the pursuit entirely.

"I just remember an analytics sort-of [report on] strengths and weaknesses, and they thought in the system we were going to play, he would be good," Cassidy recalled before a recent playoff game. "I don't want to get into all the numbers, but he'd just be a good fit—big guy, controls rebounds, makes saves he's supposed to, etc. We'd see if we could improve his game."

Cassidy's system has helped the 6-foot-6, 205-pound goalie shed the "raw prospect" tag he had carried since the Arizona Coyotes selected him in the third round of the 2015 NHL Entry Draft. Hill has ascended to a level where he doesn't look at all out of place as the backstop on a team in the Stanley Cup playoffs.

Bringing in Hill should be regarded as another masterful move by a Golden Knights' hockey operations department that has orchestrated many of them over the past year and a half. Such praise has been rare for George McPhee, president of hockey operations, and Kelly McCrimmon, general manager, after the pair seemed to fall out of favor with the majority of the fanbase last season, when the Golden Knights missed the playoffs for the only time in their history.

McPhee and McCrimmon might have made some mistakes in the past, particularly as it pertains to handling relationships with players and managing the salary cap. But they always explained that every decision was made to give the Golden Knights the best chance to win a championship.

Many questioned, and even mocked, their ability to do so, but no one should any longer. McPhee and McCrimmon have proven they can use their aggressive approach to build a championship-caliber roster.

Vegas' personnel can't be described at any lower tier than that after posting the Western Conference's best record in the regular season—the top mark in franchise history—and looking even better in the playoffs.

And the real genius of the front office might have come in the way it has made on-the-fly moves this season that appeared marginal at first but have made a major difference in the playoffs. Fan bases are often critical of their teams' trades, but there's been an extra

Golden Knights general manager Kelly McCrimmon and head coach Bruce Cassidy speak during a news conference ahead of the Stanley Cup Final. (AP Images)

level of vitriol reserved for McPhee and McCrimmon lately whenever they've made a decision.

Some called a trade-deadline deal with the St. Louis Blues for Ivan Barbashev short-sighted and graded it as a loss after the Golden Knights shipped out one of their top prospects, former first-round pick Zach Dean. Detractors accused the Golden Knights of paying for a pending free agent scorer in Barbashev who wasn't really scoring anymore.

But much like Hill's ascent under Cassidy, Barbashev has thrived in his new environs. He has raised his shooting percentage drastically in Las Vegas—19% combined between the regular season and postseason, as opposed to 11% this year in St. Louis—and scored a pair of big goals to help Vegas to a 1-0 series lead against the Edmonton Oilers in the second round.

"It was a really good deal by McCrimmon at the deadline to add that element," Cassidy said. "You need those guys in the playoffs."

The player Vegas acquired a few days after Barbashev arrived, Teddy Blueger, has also already paid off the price the Golden Knights gave to Pittsburgh for him—a third-round pick and a prospect—with a big moment of his own. Blueger scored a go-ahead goal late in the Golden Knights' eventual 4-3 overtime win against the Stars in Game 1 of the Western Conference Final.

He has centered the fourth line and given the unit the bite Cassidy craves for his depth to provide.

No discussion on recent Vegas personnel moves is complete without referencing the biggest trade in franchise history. Controversy raged early last season, when Vegas landed superstar Jack Eichel for a king's

ransom—fan favorite Alex Tuch, top prospect Peyton Krebs and a trio of draft picks.

Those who disliked the deal might have felt momentarily validated by the Golden Knights' disappointing finish last season, but a year later, Eichel is showing exactly why McPhee and McCrimmon went after him with such determination.

The hope was that the 26-year-old former No. 2 overall pick could fix the offensive woes that had held the Golden Knights back in previous playoff runs. In Game 2 against Dallas, Vegas was in an all-too-familiar offensive slog until about a quarter through the third period, when Eichel took over.

Down 2-1, the Golden Knights got an equalizing goal with under three minutes to play, when Eichel fired a no-look, behind-the-back pass to Jonathan Marchessault on a play that appropriately started when Barbashev forced a turnover. Few moments this postseason have been prettier—or a better illustration of Vegas' roster-building philosophy paying off.

Of course, given the unprecedented amount of success the Golden Knights have had since entering the league for the 2017-2018 season, McPhee and McCrimmon shouldn't need to prove their credentials to anyone. Reaching four conference finals in six years is an incredible feat. The coach has changed, as have many of the players, but the men at the top of the front office have remained constant the same throughout.

It might be uncomfortable, but they deserve a big share of the credit for the Golden Knights current heights. ■

Acquired at the trade deadline from the St. Louis Blues, Ivan Barbashev has thrived in Las Vegas. (Steve Marcus / Las Vegas Sun)

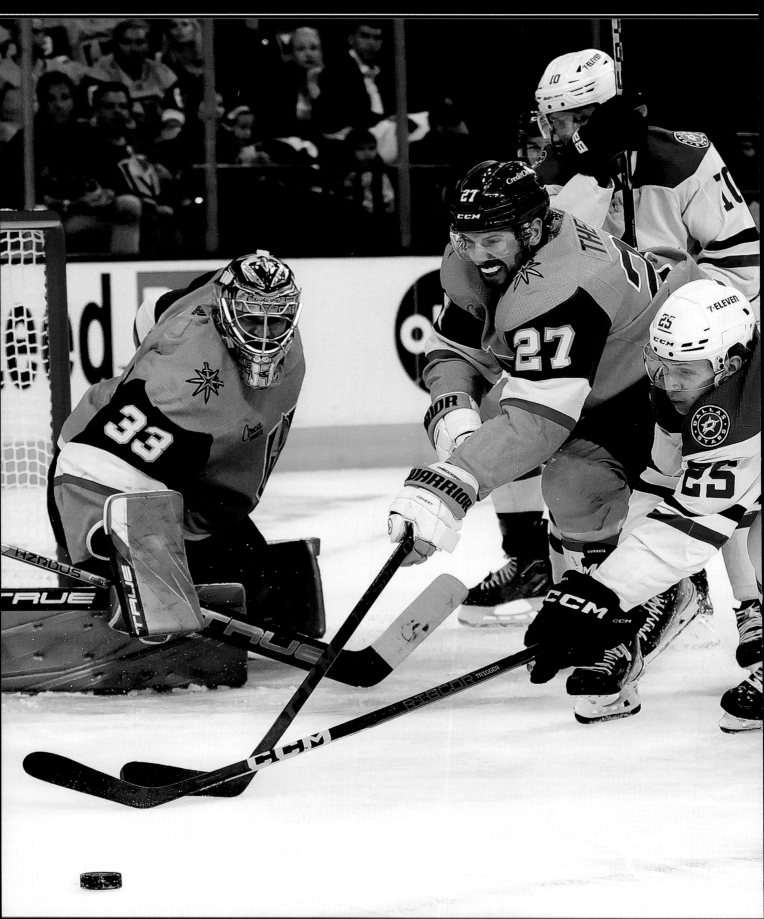

33

GOALTENDER

ADIN HILL

How the Golden Knights Goalie Became an Unlikely Playoff Hero

By Danny Webster | June 1, 2023

O fficially listed at 6-foot-4, 215 pounds, Adin Hill moves more gracefully than many goalies a fraction of that size. His side-to-side game looks effortless as he reads pucks with the calmness of a grizzled NHL veteran.

But though the 27-year-old British Columbia native has six years of experience in the league, he has appeared in just 101 games— and most of that action has been unremarkable.

Hill spent his first five seasons as a reserve on poor Arizona Coyotes and San Jose Sharks teams that never came anywhere close to the Stanley Cup Playoffs. Yet somehow, he has gone from mediocre to marvelous with the Golden Knights this year, especially during the team's postseason run.

Hill will be in the starter's crease for Vegas' Stanley Cup Final series against Florida — and he won't look out of place. The Golden Knights have reached the pinnacle of playoff hockey in large part because of what he has accomplished.

"You grow up dreaming of making the Stanley Cup Final as a kid," Hill said in Dallas after leading the Golden Knights to a series-clinching 6-0 victory over the Stars in the Western Conference Final on May 29. "It still hasn't quite sunk in yet."

Defenseman Shea Theodore clears the puck in front of goaltender Adin Hill during the Western Conference Final against the Dallas Stars. (Wade Vandervort / Las Vegas Sun)

Hill will take center stage for the Golden Knights, looking to out-duel Florida's Sergei Bobrovsky, who has drawn rave reviews for his hot play in the Panthers' series wins over Boston, Toronto and Carolina.

Hill is scorching in his own right. He made 23 saves in Vegas' decisive Game 6 victory over Dallas, his second shutout of the series.

"We kept them to the outside all night," Hill said, deflecting praise to his teammates. "It was probably my easiest game of the playoffs."

The Golden Knights went into the postseason with Laurent Brossoit as their starting goalie. He helped Vegas to a five-game series win over the Winnipeg Jets in the first round, followed by a victory in Game 1 of the second round against the Edmonton Oilers.

But Brossoit went down with a lower-body injury during the first period of Game 3, forcing Hill into action. Hill went on to stop all 24 shots he faced to help Vegas secure a win, and he hasn't slowed from there.

Hill won two of his next three starts to eliminate the Oilers, then stymied the Stars as the Golden Knights forged a 3-0 series lead they would ultimately finish off in Dallas.

"It's pretty crazy, but it's what I've dreamed about as a kid," Hill said. "We have a great team here."

The Golden Knights acquired Hill in a trade with the Sharks shortly before the season. With Robin Lehner (double hip surgery) out for the year, Vegas headed into the season with Logan Thompson and Hill as its primary goalies, while Brossoit recovered from offseason hip surgery of his own.

The unproven duo was widely considered the biggest weakness of an otherwise strong team. But Hill and Thompson proved to be a tremendous tandem, helping Vegas jump to the top of the Western Conference standings and stay there for most of the year.

Hill, who has won a grand total of 45 regular-season NHL games during his career, won 16 of those this year, including a vital 5-2-0 run after the All-Star Break, when Thompson suffered a lower-body injury to virtually end his season.

Hill then had his own setback in March, a lower-body injury that kept him out for the final month of the season. Brossoit stepped in and claimed the starting role, but Hill stayed ready once he got healthy near the start of the playoffs in case an opportunity emerged. When it did in Edmonton, he made the most of it.

He hasn't played poorly in any postseason game, including back-to-back losses to Dallas in Games 4 and 5. And instead of dwelling on those defeats, he came back stronger for Game 6, making several key saves as the Knights built their lead.

"The thing that's impressed me the most is [Hill's] poise in net," Golden Knights captain Mark Stone said. "He could have crumbled after two losses, but he realized he was playing well, so he didn't change much."

Hill has benefited greatly from his reunion with Vegas goalie coach Sean Burke, who coached Hill during his time in Arizona. It also helps that head coach Bruce Cassidy's scheme has consistently kept opponents to the outside, limiting dangerous chances.

One of the only times that defensive setup failed the Golden Knights came early in Game 6 in Edmonton. The Oilers scored two goals on their first three shots on goal, but Hill turned away the next 38 attempts to preserve the victory.

The Golden Knights have relied on depth all season long, from their forwards and defensemen to their goaltenders. Hill is one of five netminders to record a win for Vegas this season, with Jonathan Quick and Jiri Patera also seeing action amid a rash of injuries.

"He's given us a chance to win every game," forward Jonathan Marchessault said. "At this time of year, if you don't have a good goalie, I don't think you get through to the finals. You look at Bobrovsky and Hilly, they're at the top of their game. It'll be a good battle." ∎

Adin Hill stepped into the starting role following an injury to Laurent Brossoit and remained a steady presence for the Golden Knights in their championship pursuit. (Steve Marcus / Las Vegas Sun)

✦ WESTERN CONFERENCE FINAL GAME 1 ✦
May 19, 2023 • Las Vegas, Nevada
Golden Knights 4, Stars 3 (OT)

FALLEN STARS

Depth Keeps Golden Knights 'Rolling' Even Against Similar Stars

By Case Keefer

The Stars' two most prominent defensemen collided. The Golden Knights' most anonymous forward capitalized.

A third-period goal by Vegas' Teddy Blueger at T-Mobile Arena in Game 1 of the Western Conference Final was so poetic that it felt destined to wind up the game-winner in the Golden Knights' 4-3 victory.

The midseason trade acquisition was playing in only his third postseason game with the Golden Knights after having mostly been a healthy scratch in the first two rounds. And yet the former member of the Pittsburgh Penguins scored a go-ahead goal with Stars' All-Stars Miro Heiskanen and Ryan Suter tangled up helplessly beneath him, brought there mainly because of effort from fellow fourth-liner Keegan Kolesar.

It didn't end up being the decisive moment, as the Golden Knights needed an overtime winner from fellow role player Brett Howden, but each of the final two tallies illuminated the same theme. It's the Golden Knights' depth that's brought them this far, and it likely is going to be what's needed to push them over the top to reach the second Stanley Cup Final in franchise history.

"Whoever is in can do the job," Blueger said of the Golden Knights after the game. "We've got good players that can contribute up and down the lineup in different ways."

It's a minor miracle that Blueger didn't use the phrase "rolling lines" — relying on every forward group in a near-equal capacity — after Vegas muttered it approximately 10,000 times over the first month of the playoffs. The cliché far surpassed "get pucks on the net" and "play our game" as the Golden Knights' favorite idiom.

But that might have been partly, and perhaps even subconsciously, an understated insult to Vegas' first two playoff opponents — the Winnipeg Jets and Edmonton Oilers. Neither of the squads were much for "rolling lines," as they relied on star-studded groups up front.

The Stars are more like the Golden Knights in that they're depth driven. They won their first two series, against the Minnesota Wild and Seattle Kraken, by ultimately wearing down the opposition with nonstop waves of productive players.

So, in a sense, the Golden Knights and Stars have met their match in each other. Neither team will able to overwhelm the other with fresher legs constantly coming in.

It's going to come down to which fresher sets of legs outwork the other, and in Game 1, it was the ones

Golden Knights defenseman Zach Whitecloud and Dallas Stars right wing Evgenii Dadonov collide in the air during the second period of Game 1. (Wade Vandervort / Las Vegas Sun)

in gold and black over the ones in white and green.

"At the end of the day, I do believe there's a balance in all four lines (on both teams)," Vegas coach Bruce Cassidy said before Game 1. "So that could work either way. That could be one thing you talk about that one team got caught up in or vice versa."

Dallas got caught up on Friday. The Stars' best forwards were better than the Golden Knights' best forwards, as each of the visitors' top three goal-scorers from the regular season — Jason Robertson, Roope Hintz and Jamie Benn — found the back of the net.

None of Vegas' top seven goal-scorers from the regular season did the same. The Golden Knights' top two lines were shut out in regulation, with William Karlsson the lone big name creating highlights with a pair of goals for the third group.

That scoring split would spell defeat for most teams this deep into the playoffs. Just not Vegas.

Consider Dallas coach Pete DeBoer unsurprised. It's not much unlike the strategy he deployed over the previous three seasons behind the Golden Knights' bench.

DeBoer wasn't satisfied with his new team's series-opening performance, but he was also far from panicked after coming back from Game 1 overtime losses in each of the first two rounds.

"Seattle had that type of team too and actually scored more than Vegas scores and we found ways during that series to shut them down," DeBoer said. "We've got to find a way. We've got to be better than we were tonight is the bottom line."

"The good news is, the other two (series) ended the right way so that's what we'll hope for."

Howden ended Game 1 95 seconds into overtime when he recovered a pass he initially mishandled off the boards and fired it into the back of Dallas goalie Jake Oettinger's skates and into the the goal. Maybe Howden

was the more appropriate final hero, or at least one on par with Blueger.

The former New York Ranger was just as unknown as Blueger upon being traded to the Golden Knights before last season. He's been an off-and-on contributor ever since but has really proven valuable to Vegas in these playoffs, most recently next to team captain Mark Stone.

Howden had never scored an overtime goal and hadn't chipped in with a game-winner all season.

Stopping players like Howden and Blueger from having their moment is every bit as important for opponents as slowing Stone and Jack Eichel.

Dallas is best-equipped to do so out of every team Vegas has seen in the playoffs to this point, but it's off to an 0-for-1 start.

So far, Vegas is outrolling them.

"I think that's the coolest thing about our team, that we have so much depth up front and on the back end and obviously in goaltending too," Howden said. "I just think we have a really deep team and can really roll our lines however we want on any given night." ∎

Reilly Smith and Dallas Stars defenseman Joel Hanley vie for the puck during the first period. (Wade Vandervort / Las Vegas Sun)

FINISH STRONG

Stephenson Overcomes Early Struggles to Win Game 2 for Golden Knights

By Danny Webster

The redemption arc for Chandler Stephenson was a roller coaster in Game 2. He took two uncharacteristic penalties. One of the best faceoff winners in the league, he had his worst performance all season. He had one shot on goal on a night where the Golden Knights struggled to find offense.

But that one shot is why the Golden Knights are two wins away from making the Stanley Cup Final.

Stephenson scored 1:12 into overtime for the first Stanley Cup Playoff winner of his career, and the Golden Knights rallied to defeat the Dallas Stars 3-2 at T-Mobile Arena, giving Vegas a 2-0 series lead.

"Any time you're watching the playoffs growing up, getting a game-winner, it's pretty special," Stephenson said. "It hasn't really hit me yet that it's happened, but it's cool."

For the second straight game, the Golden Knights went to overtime, ended it in less than two minutes, and Stephenson's line was on the ice for the winner both times. Brett Howden scored 1:35 into the extra session to win Game 1 at home.

It was a different finish than Howden's goal, but the mentality was the same with Stephenson. Shea Theodore's shot from above the right circle was kicked away by Dallas goalie Jake Oettinger, but Stephenson was alone on the weak side to score his first goal since Game 3 of the second-round series against Edmonton.

Mark Stone scored a power-play goal, and Jonathan Marchessault scored the game-tying goal with 2:22 remaining in regulation to give the Golden Knights a chance in the extra frame. Adin Hill won his fourth straight start with 26 saves.

The series now shifts to Dallas for Game 3, and the Golden Knights are 4-1 on the road this postseason.

"They're tight games and we know what type of team Dallas is," Marchessault said. "We're a veteran group. We know how to handle those situations."

Singling out Stephenson doesn't seem right in a game where the Golden Knights couldn't generate anything offensively. They had 10 shots on goal through two periods as Dallas adjusted defensively by shutting down any entries toward the offensive blue line.

But the first-time All-Star, who now has 13 points

Chandler Stephenson scored the overtime winner in Game 2 for the Golden Knights, who fought their way to a 2-0 series lead. (AP Images)

through the Golden Knights' 13 playoff games, struggled by his standards. Stephenson was one of the best in the league at faceoffs this season, winning 58.3% of draws taken, and went 2 of 15 on Sunday.

His line — with Mark Stone and Brett Howden — combined for four shots on goal at 5-on-5.

Stephenson took two uncharacteristic penalties; a slashing call on Dallas' Roope Hintz in the first period that didn't need to happen, and then a cross-checking call in retaliation to defenseman Colin Miller tangling with him near the Vegas bench.

"There's obviously emotion," Stephenson said. "The more it goes on, the more emotion there is. I need to keep my emotions in check. You never want to give a good power play two opportunities."

For a team that's gone 10-3 in the playoffs, the Golden Knights do better when they're trailing early. They gave up the opening goal for the 10th time in 13 games. Dallas defenseman Miro Heiskanen opened the scoring at 2:47 for a 1-0 lead.

Stone capitalized on a 5-on-3 following subsequent penalties from the Stars' third defense pairing of Thomas Harley and Joel Hanley. Stone received a pass in front from Stephenson and beat Oettinger to tie it 1-1.

The Golden Knights' penalty-killing unit looked strong through its first three tests against the Dallas power play. Outside of Dallas' first power play in Game 1, the Vegas PK handled the Pete DeBoer-coached man advantage, having played in that system for three years when DeBoer was Vegas' coach.

Marchessault was called for tripping in the offensive zone in the second period, which led to Dallas' Jason Robertson scoring for the second straight game and a 2-1 lead at 9:21 of the period.

Following 50 minutes of the Stars playing near-shutdown defense, the Golden Knights started to find a rhythm offensively, led by center Jack Eichel. His pace in the final half of the third period started opening the ice for his linemates.

That came to fruition on Marchessault's game-tying goal. It started with Eichel sending the puck behind the Dallas net. Eichel received a pass from Ivan Barbashev, then did a no-look drop pass to Marchessault cutting in the slot to tie it 2-2.

It woke up the Golden Knights' forecheck, and that play carried over to overtime where Stephenson's goal sent the crowd of 18,358 into a frenzy.

"It wasn't our best game," Stephenson said. "Once Marchy scored, it brought a lot of life into us."

In a postseason run where no win has been considered "ugly," this was the ugliest of them all. Despite it being a far cry from the dominant offensive game they played in Game 1, the Golden Knights' resiliency showed yet again with their eighth come-from-behind win.

As for the game puck for Stephenson's game-winner, his son Ford is about to turn 1 year old. The puck is going in his room.

Stephenson started slow, but finished strong in an emphatic way. And his goal is why the Golden Knights are in the driver's seat.

"He's been awesome all postseason long," Eichel said. "He's one of the more underrated players in our league. I don't think he's talked about enough, but he does it for us every night and I think everyone in this room looks at him as one of the better players in the world." ∎

Mark Stone scored on a pass from Chandler Stephenson to even the score after the Golden Knights gave up an early goal just minutes into the first period. (Steve Marcus / Las Vegas Sun)

COOLER HEADS PREVAIL

Hill's Shutout, Golden Knights' Game Plan Put Them One Win from Finals

By Danny Webster

Among the things Adin Hill stopped in Game 3: 34 pucks and a bag of popcorn. Nothing is fazing Hill. Whether it be pucks or buttery goodness, he remains on a level worthy of leading the Golden Knights to the Stanley Cup Final.

He's one win away from that.

Hill made 34 saves and recorded the first playoff shutout of his career, and the Golden Knights defeated the Dallas Stars 4-0 to take a commanding 3-0 lead in the best-of-seven Western Conference Final.

"It speaks volumes to our team, too," Hill said. "We haven't lost many games in these playoffs. We're on a roll and we're playing well defensively."

And a weird series it has become in the span of four days. A battle between two of the West's top teams started with consecutive overtime wins, won by the Golden Knights, suggesting that this could be a tight series.

But it took 7:10 for Game 3 to flip on its head with the Golden Knights jumping out to a 3-0 lead with goals from Jonathan Marchessault, Ivan Barbashev and William Carrier. Falling behind was the least of Dallas' worries, though.

Stars captain Jamie Benn was called for a major penalty and given a game misconduct less than two minutes in after cross-checking Vegas captain Mark Stone who was lying on the ice. Benn, normally a well-respected player, lost the cool for his group while the game was still in its infancy.

Benn did not speak to the media after the game.

"He made a mistake. He feels really bad about it. I'm not going to pile on him," Stars coach Pete DeBoer said. "He leads by example every day on and off the ice. Fortunately, Mark Stone is OK, and we've got to live with the consequences."

That set the tone for a frustrating night for the Stars, capped off by 5-foot-9 forward Max Domi getting called for minor penalties of cross-checking and roughing, and given a 10-minute misconduct for taking a charge at 6-foot-6 Golden Knights defenseman Nic Hague. The fans inside American Airlines Center responded to the call by throwing trash onto the ice with 21.6 seconds remaining in the second period.

The situation was so tense, and the ice littered beyond casual clean-up duty, that the period ended early and the 21.6 seconds would be resumed following the second intermission.

Nicolas Hague competes for control of the puck against Dallas Stars defenseman Miro Heiskanen. (AP Images)

As Hill and the Golden Knights came back onto the ice, a bag of popcorn bounced off the goalie's mask.

"I guess everything was just hitting me tonight," Hill said with a laugh.

Right now, there's one team laughing. The other is in danger.

The Golden Knights are one win away from advancing to the Stanley Cup Final for the second time in franchise history. It's a playoff run in which the Golden Knights have won 11 of 14 games, with a 5-1 road record while outscoring opponents 23-13 away from T-Mobile Arena, and pristine goaltending during a five-game winning streak.

Vegas has frustrated teams at every turn and has done so in all facets. The Golden Knights are scoring 3.71 goals per game and giving up just 2.71. They've allowed 10 total goals during this five-game winning streak, a combination of strong team defense and Hill's effort since coming in for Laurent Brossoit in Game 3 in Edmonton.

Hill is now 6-1 in eight appearances. His .940 save percentage and 1.96 goals allowed are Conn Smythe-worthy. Only Florida's Sergei Bobrovsky is on a level of equal brilliance.

"I do know what we're doing is we're making it hard for them to get inside and get good chances," coach Bruce Cassidy said. "Our style of play is to protect the middle of the ice. We're not always on top of our game, but how we want to play, the players are receptive to that and they have been."

Not a single person would've blamed Vegas for retaliating after what Benn did to Stone.

Then again, that's what the Stars would've wanted. A desperate team trailing by two games would want to steal momentum in any way. But when Benn cross-checked Stone, the Dallas captain was the lone one to enter the box.

That came 42 seconds after Marchessault opened the scoring to give the Golden Knights a 1-0 lead. As Benn's penalty neared its end, Barbashev scored at 5:57 for a 2-0 lead. Carrier added his 1:13 later to chase Dallas goalie Jake Oettinger out of the game.

The Golden Knights didn't respond with physical retaliation. They let their play dictate the night.

"You keep your composure," defenseman Alex Pietrangelo said. "You've got a five-minute power play. We know we wanted to get at least one, and we did."

Pietrangelo's goal at 8:28 of the second period capped off an offensive night that saw four goals on 16 shots.

The Stars tried, with as limited resources at their disposal, to make a game out of it. With Benn already out, the Stars then lost forward Evgenii Dadonov to injury in the first period and played the remainder of the game with 10 forwards.

Meanwhile, no team has ever blown a 3-0 lead in the round before the Stanley Cup Final (46-0). The Clarence S. Campbell Bowl will be in the building for Game 4. The Golden Knights are one win away from putting an emphatic stamp on an impressive run through the Western Conference playoffs.

None of that matters until they get the fourth win. That first chance comes in less than 48 hours. ∎

Adin Hill blocks a shot by Dallas Stars defenseman Joel Hanley during the second period, one of Hill's 34 saves on the night. (AP Images)

CLOSING TIME

Golden Knights Fail to Clinch Against Stars, Lose Game 4 in Overtime

By Danny Webster

The Clarence S. Campbell Bowl will be getting on a plane to Las Vegas, but not yet in the possession of the Golden Knights.

The Western Conference Final will see a fifth game.

The Dallas Stars staved off elimination thanks to Joe Pavelski's game-winning overtime goal 3:18 into the extra frame, and the Golden Knights lost 3-2 in Game 4 at American Airlines Center.

The series reached overtime for the third time in four games. The Golden Knights won Games 1 and 2 each less than two minutes into the fourth period. This time, Pavelski's first goal of the series allowed the Stars to live another day, despite being down captain Jamie Benn (suspension) and forward Evgenii Dadonov (lower-body injury).

"Give them credit," coach Bruce Cassidy said. "They did what they had to do."

Jonathan Marchessault and William Karlsson scored, and Adin Hill made 39 saves for his first loss in six starts in the Golden Knights' first defeat since Game 4 of the second round against Edmonton on May 10.

The fourth win is always the most difficult in a series. Those celebrating in the streets of Sunrise, Fla., right now would tend to disagree after the eighth-seeded Florida Panthers completed a sweep of the Carolina Hurricanes in the Eastern Conference Final.

But with the Golden Knights trying to close it out on the road, they knew Dallas' best game was coming after getting shut out 4-0 in Game 3. Vegas even scored first for the second consecutive game — the first time all postseason that's happened — when Karlsson scored 4:17 into the game for a 1-0 lead.

Even without Benn and Dadonov, the Stars found something that worked, especially on the rush. Dallas dominated in scoring chances (27-16) and high-danger chances (12-8) through two periods.

"There was a lot of rush chances," forward Reilly Smith said. "I don't think we did a good enough job making it difficult on them."

Giving the Stars power plays aided in that process. Brayden McNabb committed both Vegas penalties in the game, and both led to power-play goals. Jason Robertson scored his first of two at 15:42 of the first period to tie it 1-1.

After Marchessault scored his sixth goal in five games to restore the Vegas lead at 2-1, Robertson scored his fourth of the series at 17:21 to tie it 2-2.

While Hill had another night where he looked unbeatable, Dallas goalie Jake Oettinger returned to form with his best performance of the series. Oettinger made 37 saves less than two days after allowing three goals in 7:10 before being pulled.

Both goalies were great, but the playoffs are only

Left wing William Carrier drives to the net against Dallas Stars goaltender Jake Oettinger during the second period of Game 4 in Dallas. (AP Images)

remembered for the last goal given up. McNabb was called for his second high-sticking penalty at 2:28 of overtime, and Pavelski's one-timer from the left circle beat Hill 50 seconds later.

"He's been so good for us, it's not fair to let him down in a situation like that," said Marchessault about Hill, who is the third goalie in team history to win five straight starts (Marc-Andre Fleury, Laurent Brossoit).

The onus certainly won't go on Hill, especially for making 10-bell saves to keep the Golden Knights in it until the end. That included a breakaway stop on Fredrik Olofsson late in regulation.

Marchessault said the effort level in this close-out game wasn't good enough against a desperate team. He credited the Stars' forecheck for giving the Golden Knights fits, which led to rough breakouts from the defensive zone.

"Closing a series, it's probably the hardest game of the series," Marchessault said. "Not good enough."

Considering the Golden Knights escaped with two wins at home that needed overtime, getting a split in Dallas was an equally positive scenario, even up 3-0 in the series. While there is understandable disappointment from Marchessault and Smith to not close it out, the Golden Knights get a chance to finish things on home ice.

"We're trying to play the right way, but the desperation was a little higher than ours," Marchessault said. "This time of the year, it's not about X's and O's. It's about who wants it more. I thought they wanted it more than we did." ∎

MOUNTING PRESSURE

Golden Knights Implode in Third Period, Can't Close Series with Stars

By Danny Webster

Desperation is something the Dallas Stars have learned to play with the last two games. It's worked.

It might be time for the Golden Knights to find that level of anguish because the pressure is starting to mount.

Vegas gave up two goals in the third period of a tie game, allowing the Stars to win 4-2 in Game 5 of the Western Conference Final at T-Mobile Arena and extend the series at least one more game.

Suddenly, a commanding 3-0 series lead for the Golden Knights has shrunk to 3-2. They'll be getting on a plane for Dallas to play Game 6 and will get a third opportunity to try and make the Stanley Cup Final.

"I don't think we've brought our best the last two games, but we've still been in a good spot to win the game," said Golden Knights captain Mark Stone. "Definitely got to bring a better effort and start playing more desperate with a chance to wrap it up."

Chandler Stephenson and Ivan Barbashev scored, and Adin Hill made 30 saves as the Golden Knights lost consecutive games in the playoffs for the first time this postseason.

Considering what the Stars were up against these last two games, it shouldn't have been difficult for the Golden Knights to reach that level of desperation.

The Stars trailed 3-0 in a series where they weren't going to have captain Jamie Benn in the lineup for two games after cross-checking Stone in Game 3, and would be without reliable top-nine forward Evgenii Dadonov.

In Game 4, it was Dallas' top line of Jason Robertson, Joe Pavelski and Roope Hintz making the difference. Saturday was Dallas' depth on display.

Ty Dellandrea scored twice, both coming within a 1:27 span in the third period, and fourth-line forward Luke Glendening scored for Dallas. Robertson also scored for his fifth goal in the series after having two in the first two rounds.

And each goal proved more vital than the next.

Glendening's came 1:48 after Barbashev's opening goal at 13:36 of the first period. The quick response silenced the eighth-largest crowd ever at T-Mobile Arena of 18,546 in a sudden hurry.

The same script happened in the second period. Stephenson's goal at 3:20 of the second was immediately answered by Robertson at 5:29 to tie it 2-2.

"They had good pushback," coach Bruce Cassidy said. "We got the lead, they answered right away."

The Golden Knights couldn't find their own version of pushback. Every time the Stars answered, the Golden Knights failed to have consistent stretches of success. Dallas turned the game in its favor with puck possession and extended time in the offensive zone.

Ivan Barbashev scores during the Golden Knights' 4-2 loss to the Stars. (Wade Vandervort / Las Vegas Sun)

Dallas took the lead at 10:35 when Dellandrea's shot deflected off Alex Pietrangelo's stick and trickled by Hill, giving the Stars their first lead at 3-2. At 12:02, a loose puck off a scramble in front found its way to Dellandrea, making it 4-2.

On a night where Hill made highlight-reel saves to keep the Golden Knights in it, his teammates let him down.

"He played well," Stone said. "He doesn't let in any bad goals, knock on wood. He's given us a chance every game we've been in."

The Golden Knights have usually been a good team at taking care of the puck, but they had 24 giveaways on Saturday. One of them led directly to Dellandrea's second goal.

"We had 24 giveaways. I'm not sure you're beating the Arizona Coyotes in January with 24 giveaways," Cassidy said. "No disrespect to Arizona, but it's not the right way to play."

Cassidy's vantage point showed Dellandrea's first goal was one he should've stopped, but it was on Hill's teammates to pick him up in response.

Less than two minutes later, the Golden Knights found themselves going from celebrating and preparing for the Stanley Cup Final, to now still needing one more win to get there.

Now, the Stars will have reinforcements when they return home to American Airlines Center. Benn will return after serving his two-game suspension, and the Stars will carry momentum as wide as East Texas with their captain back in the lineup.

Hill has done his part in every game. The Golden Knights will need one more stellar performance from their goalie going back on the road Monday, but that desperation will need to be followed by production. Stone doesn't have a point in three games. Jack Eichel has yet to score a goal this series.

If there's anything else that needs to change for Vegas heading into Game 6, that would be it.

"You like your chances when you're going into the third tied to win a series," Stone said, "but we've got to regroup, refocus and get ready for Game 6." ∎

FLAWLESS

Vegas Dominates Dallas in Game 6 to Reach the Stanley Cup Final

By Danny Webster

Jonathan Marchessault had a feeling. He called it like Joe Namath guaranteeing the New York Jets would win Super Bowl III or Mark Messier doubling down on the New York Rangers rallying from down 3-2 to win the 1994 Stanley Cup.

"We're going to come out here and play one of our best road games," Marchessault said following morning skate ahead of Game 6.

What transpired for three hours at American Airlines Center later that night wasn't just one of the best road games for the Golden Knights — it might have been their best game all season. And it happened at the perfect time, with a 6-0 win over the Stars in Game 6 of the Western Conference Final sending Vegas to the Stanley Cup Final for the second time in franchise history.

"I just knew we were going to show up tonight and give a good battle," Marchessault said after the game. "I think everyone's brain was turned on tonight."

It's difficult to say a team can play a perfect game from start to finish, let alone in the playoffs. One bad bounce can end a shutout, or a defensive lapse can turn a great night into something less. But there are instances far and few between that can be classified as flawless.

The 60-minute effort the Golden Knights put together fits into that category.

The Stars turned a 3-0 series deficit into 3-2 in the blink of an eye. If the Golden Knights lost and had to go back to Las Vegas for Game 7, the pressure would be astronomical. Stars coach Pete DeBoer, the former Vegas coach, has never lost a Game 7.

But the Golden Knights were one of the best road teams all season. They were tied with the New Jersey Devils for 60 points earned away from home, trailing only the Boston Bruins (64).

They got to that point by believing in their depth as a four-line team with three reliable defense pairings. It didn't take long for the Golden Knights to find their stride in Game 6 as William Carrier opened the scoring at 3:41 of the opening period, the beginning of a three-goal first period.

Coach Bruce Cassidy went back to the line combinations that put Vegas at its best. He moved Nic Roy back to fourth-line center between Carrier and Keegan Kolesar. That trio has been the best fourth-line combination all season. Following William Karlsson's first of two goals on the night — a power-play tally at 10:25 for a 2-0 lead — the fourth line got rewarded again when Kolesar made it 3-0 at 14:00.

Adin Hill made a save during the second period of Game 6, part of an impeccable team effort that earned the Golden Knights a Stanley Cup Final berth. (AP Images)

"We knew exactly what we wanted to bring right off the bat," Carrier said. "Good for us to get those goals."

Much like Game 3, it was a dominant first 20 minutes. The biggest difference was Stars captain Jamie Benn — who returned after serving a two-game suspension — didn't get tossed this game. The Stars operated at full strength and still looked overwhelmed.

Vegas' breakouts and zone entries were also near flawless. Puck movement was at its best. The postgame numbers say the Golden Knights had 11 giveaways, but it didn't look like it.

Even when shot volume was toned down in the final two periods, the Golden Knights still made the most of their chances. Marchessault scored on Vegas' first shot of the second period at 10:25, pushing the lead to 4-0. Karlsson's second goal came in the third period, with Michael Amadio also scoring.

Adin Hill recorded his second shutout of the series with 23 saves, pushing the Golden Knights' record to 12-5 in the postseason.

"Boy, if we can bottle that going forward, we'll be a tough team to beat," coach Bruce Cassidy said. "Guys responded well to a little adversity. Great start, and we just kept going from there."

Evening getting out to a 3-0 start in the first period, "you still have to push," captain Mark Stone said. "When Marchessault got that fourth one, then you start to feel, OK, we're playing a really good game here."

The performance was a reminder of why the Golden Knights earned the top seed in the Western Conference and how they battled to earn home-ice advantage throughout the playoffs.

"I think they played a perfect elimination game," said DeBoer, who coached the Golden Knights the

William Carrier opened the scoring for the Golden Knights in the first period. Vegas' fourth line of Carrier, Nicolas Roy and Keegan Kolesar was responsible for two goals in the 6-0 victory. (AP Images)

previous three seasons, adding that there are many in the Vegas locker room he hopes win the Stanley Cup.

The clinching win means there will be a Stanley Cup Final game played at T-Mobile Arena for the first time since 2018, when the Golden Knights took the sports world by storm and came within three wins of the Stanley Cup in their inaugural season.

Only six players — Carrier, Karlsson, Marchessault, Reilly Smith, Brayden McNabb and Shea Theodore — were part of the on-ice roster in that five-game loss to the Washington Capitals.

Now, six years in, Vegas has a veteran group that has overcome adversity — the seven-game collapse in 2019 against San Jose; losing to Dallas in the 2020 conference final; falling flat in 2021 against Montreal; missing the playoffs for the first time last season. All of that has led to one more shot at the Cup.

"We had an honest conversation last night about what's in front of us," Cassidy said. "We took another step and we got through this to the final. Now, the conversation becomes about finishing the job."

"It's a great accomplishment to be the best team in the Western Conference, but we want to be the best team in the league," Stone said. "We've got to get ready to play the Florida Panthers. This is a great achievement, but we want the Stanley Cup." ∎

Bill Daly, deputy commissioner of the NHL, presents the Clarence S. Campbell Bowl to Vegas' Reilly Smith, Mark Stone and Alex Pietrangelo. (AP Images)

81

FORWARD

JONATHAN MARCHESSAULT

A Full-Fledged Golden Knights Legend
Amid Another Dominant Playoff Run

By Case Keefer | June 1, 2023

J onathan Marchessault swung his left leg out after the first
yelled staring down at the ice following the second, and lau
an uppercut through the air on the third.

And the veteran Golden Knights' forward apparently w
done celebrating his natural hat trick—three straight goals
second period of a 5-2 Game 6 victory to eliminate the Edmonton Oile
saved some more emotional outbursts for the visiting locker room at I
Place in Edmonton after the contest.

"Good for [Marchessault, but] we're going to have to hear it for t
next four or five days," Golden Knights coach Bruce Cassidy joked du
in his post-game news conference. "That's the unfortunate part, but
live with that."

Four or five days? Try another couple of weeks, because there's be
reason for Marchessault to tone down his bravado so far.

The 32-year-old brought the red-hot form he found against Edmo
into the Western Conference Final against Dallas, during which he had
goals—and at least one point in each of the final five games.

Throughout the playoffs, Marchessault has arguably been Vegas' n
valuable skater.

Jonathan Marchessault overcame a first-round slump to become one of
the Golden Knights' most productive players during their playoff run. (Wade
Vandervort / Las Vegas Sun)

ke playing this time of year," Marchessault said
spatching Dallas. "Regular season, yeah, it's fun,
ike more of a routine. The passion is there, and
t to score goals is there. But in the playoffs, it's
animal. That's what fuels me."
nis all sounds eerily familiar, it's because it has
happened before. Marchessault similarly raised
e to a lethal level during the Golden Knights'
on-season Stanley Cup Final run in 2018, with
ompanying moxie to match.
hat year's Western Conference Final against
eg, he was showing up for home games at
e Arena in a customized Golden Knights'
rghini—and getting then-coach Gerard Gallant to
nately refer to him as "a cocky little guy."
rchessault also set the NHL record for most
by a player for a team in its first playoff
ance with 21, eight goals and 13 assists.
ere's Marchy again," Cassidy said of
ssault's ability to come through in the biggest
ts. "I don't know the entire history. I delved into it
d into it, but now I've seen it with my own eyes."
e only material Cassidy needed to read to realize
archessault has meant to the franchise overall
ecord book, where No. 81 sits first in the vast
y of career offensive categories. That includes
-season goals, regular-season points, postseason
nd postseason points.
bad for a "little guy" the Panthers willingly gave
the Golden Knights' Expansion Draft, reportedly
e of concerns over his 5-foot-9, 174-pound frame
ability to contribute as an all-around player.
rchessault isn't the only "Original Misfit" still
roster—Karlsson, Reilly Smith, William Carrier,
n McNabb and Shea Theodore were all also
d through the expansion draft—but no one
epresents what the Golden Knights have stood
e the beginning.

And no one has been more impactful in Vegas.
Marchessault might not be as naturally talented as
Eichel or Mark Stone, or even as beloved as original
goalie Marc-André Fleury, but he has accomplished
more than anyone during his time here.

"It's been a roller coaster six years for sure, a lot of
ups and downs," Marchessault said. "I'm definitely really
proud of that term [Original Misfits]. That's something
we started. We were a bunch of nobodies ... and we still
have a chip on our shoulder. We're going to keep going
until our organization wins the ultimate goal."

For as much as teammates and coaches like
to joke about Marchessault's brash personality,
he hasn't shown that side of himself in front of
the media much lately. He has largely credited his
playoff success to others, describing multiple goals
as "lucky" and a byproduct of playing alongside "an
amazing player" like Eichel.

He has also continually resisted looking forward,
emphasizing staying in the moment no matter how
promising things have looked for the Golden Knights.
Marchessault said he wasn't as grounded during the
Golden Knights' 2018 Stanley Cup Final run.

He was so sure the team would win the
championship, he was left shocked when things began
to go wrong against the Washington Capitals, who beat
the Golden Knights in five games.

"It's one of those things that kind of slipped away
from us that year," Marchessault said. "I know I've
learned from my mistakes."

Still, don't be surprised if Marchessault's calm
crumbles should the Golden Knights capture the Stanley
Cup. Who knows what type of celebration the greatest
Golden Knight of all might think up, should such
triumphs materialize.

"I always try to keep the momentum up, keep
everybody happy," Marchessault said. "To be honest, it's
been one of those years that we have fun every day." ∎

an Marchessault has been with the Golden Knights since the franchise's expansion draft and has now led them to
t Stanley Cup. (Wade Vandervort / Las Vegas Sun)

Steve Marcus / Las Vegas Sun